SAINTS FOR BOYS

# A SAINT
## FOR YOUR NAME

Albert J. Nevins, M.M.

ILLUSTRATED BY JAMES McILRATH

D0770073

Our Sunday Visitor, Inc.
Huntington, Indiana 46750

# A
# SAINT
# FOR YOUR NAME

ISBN: 0-87973-320-9
Library of Congress Catalog Card Number: 79-92504

Published, printed, and bound in the United States of America

# In This Book:

## Pictures

# Before You Begin

It is a Christian custom that when a child is baptized it is given the name of a saint who is to be a protector and model for the new Christian. Later at Confirmation the child chooses to take the name of another saint who is also a protector and model.

Since there are many thousands of saints, this book lists only those whose names seem more popular. There are also different forms of the same name and different ways to spell a name. These are found in the list in the back of the book. Often there is more than one saint with the same name, and the book lists only those best known.

After each saint's name is the language from which the name comes and its meaning in that language. The date given after each name is the feast day of the saint, and thus it is also the name or feast day of those who have the name of the saint. Such a day should be treated something like a birthday — a special day on which you should be remembered and you should remember your saint.

This book has only names of boys. There is another book for girls.

It is hoped that you will try to become like the saint after whom you have been named, remembering the saint in your prayers and imitating his love for Jesus. Your saint lived a life pleasing to God. With his help and your own efforts, you can do the same.

# Part One:

# Saints for Boys

*(alphabetical listing)*

*ABRAHAM*

# Aaron (*Hebrew:* Lofty Mountain)                     June 21

The name Aaron first appears in the Bible in the Book of Exodus.
Aaron was the brother of Moses and a member of the tribe of Levi. With
Moses he shared in the leadership of the people and often spoke in the
name of Moses. Like Moses, he never entered the Promised Land but died
on the slopes of Mount Hor. He was the first High Priest of the Israelites
and was succeeded by his son.

# Abraham (*Hebrew:* Father of Many)                     Oct. 9

## Other Forms: Abram

About 2,000 years before Christ, there lived a chieftain near the city
of Ur in the land of the Chaldeans (Mesopotamia), whose name was
Abram, which means "God is exalted." Abram was different from the
people among whom he lived because, while they worshiped many gods,
he worshiped the one, true God. Because of this, he was pleasing to God.
One day he heard God's voice within himself saying, "Go forth from the
land of your relatives to a land I will show you. I will bless you and make
of you a great nation." Abram obeyed God and with his family and his
flocks made the long journey to the land of Canaan, which today we know
as Israel. God was pleased that Abram obeyed him and he changed
Abram's name to Abraham, which means "father of many."

God had promised Abraham that his descendants would be as many
as the stars in the sky. Abraham did not know how this was to happen
since he and his wife, Sarah, had no children. Then, unexpectedly, God
sent Abraham a son whom he named Isaac. He loved the boy greatly, and
it was through Isaac that God was to test Abraham once more.

Again Abraham heard the voice of God. It said: "Abraham, take your
son Isaac, your only one, whom you love, and offer him up as a sacrifice on
a hill I will show you." Abraham was sad but he prepared to obey God. He
took Isaac to the hill, made ready a fire, tied the boy and laid him on the
logs. He was ready to light the fire when a voice spoke from heaven, telling
him to wait. The voice said that Abraham had proven his love for God by
his willingness to give up his son. Isaac did not have to die. Once again
God blessed Abraham and promised that he would be the father of a great
people. Abraham is the ancestor of the Jewish and Arab peoples. He died
at a very old age and was buried with his wife in a cave.

Some other saints with this name:

St. Abraham Kidunaia (Mesopotamia) *Mar. 16*
St. Abraham of Carrhae (Syria) *Feb. 14*
St. Abraham of Kratia (Syria) *Dec. 6*
St. Abraham of Rostov (Russia) *Oct. 29*
St. Abraham of Smolensk (Russia) *Aug. 21*

11

# Adam (*Hebrew:* First of Earth) Dec. 24

### Another Form: Adan

The Bible names Adam as the first human being on earth. He was created by God in a very special way. God also created Eve to be his wife and companion. God tested Adam and Eve, and because they failed the test, they lost, not only for themselves but for all mankind, many gifts which God would have given them. He is one of the patrons of gardeners.

Another saint with this name:

Bl. Adam of Loccum (Germany) *Dec. 22*

# Adrian (*Greek:* Brave) Sept. 8

### Other Forms: Adrien, Hadrian

Adrian was a Roman officer (c. 300 A.D.) who was stationed in what is now Turkey. One day 23 Christians were arrested and were beaten and tortured by the soldiers. Adrian was so moved by their suffering and bravery that he stepped forward and said: "Count me with these men, for I am also a Christian." Adrian was immediately arrested. Along with other Christians, he was sentenced to have his arms and legs broken and then cut off. He died during the torture. Later the broken bodies were ordered burned, but a heavy rainstorm came up and put out the fire. Christians gathered the remains of Adrian and his companions and buried them. Later the relics were taken to Rome. Adrian became a very popular martyr and was named the patron of soldiers.

# Alan (*Celtic:* Harmony) Sept. 8

### Other Forms: Alain, Allan, Allen

Blessed Alan de la Roche was born in the Brittany area of France and from his earliest years had a great love of and devotion to the Virgin Mary. He entered the Dominican Order and soon won a reputation as a brilliant student. After being ordained a priest, he was assigned to promote devotion both to the Virgin Mary and the Rosary. He preached in France, Belgium, Denmark, and Holland. While working in Holland, he was taken ill on the Feast of the Assumption (Aug. 15) and died there on the Feast of the Nativity of the Blessed Virgin (Sept. 8), 1475.

# Alban *(Latin:* White)  June 22

**Other Forms: Alben, Albin, Alva**

St. Alban was the first martyr of Britain. He was converted to Christianity by a priest to whom he had given shelter. He was arrested during the persecution of Diocletian (about 303) at Verulam, later renamed after him, where a famous abbey was built to his honor. He converted one of his jailers, who also died with him.

# Albert *(Teutonic:* Illustrious)  Nov. 15

**Other Forms: Adalbert, Alberto, Albrecht, Bert, Delbert**

St. Albert the Great is one of the most famous teachers of Christianity. He was born into a wealthy and powerful family in Germany which had big plans for him. Over their strong objections, Albert decided to become a priest and entered the Dominican Order in Italy. His brilliance and scholarship caused his superiors to send him to the University of Paris to teach and get his master's degree. Students flocked to his classes, and one of them, Thomas of Aquino, was to become an equally great philosopher and also a saint. Albert returned to Cologne, where he continued to teach and write. There his reputation for learning became so great that he was called Albert the Great even in his own lifetime. Against his objections he was made a bishop. He died in his eighties on Nov. 15, 1280. He was named a saint, a Doctor of the Church, and patron of scientists and philosophers.

Some other saints with this name:

St. Albert of Cashel (Ireland) *Jan. 19*
St. Albert of Jerusalem *Sept. 25*
St. Albert of Louvain (Belgium) *Nov. 21*
St. Albert of Ponteda (Italy) *Sept. 12*

# Alcuin *(Teutonic:* Noble Friend)  May 19

Blessed Alcuin was born in York, England, and became the head of a school there, winning a reputation as a scholar and teacher. He made several visits to Rome, and on one of them the Emperor Charlemagne invited him to become an adviser at the royal court. Later, Charlemagne appointed him head of a Benedictine abbey in France where he continued his teaching and attracted many students both from France and England. He died in 804.

*ST. ALBERT THE GREAT*

14

# Alexander (*Greek:* Helper of Men)    Dec. 1

**Other Forms: Alistair, Alec, Alex, Alejandro, Sacha, Sandor**

Alexander Bryant was a popular and handsome student at Oxford University during the persecution of the Catholic Church by Queen Elizabeth. Like most of the students, he had abandoned his Catholic religion in favor of the Anglican Church. However, while at Oxford, through the efforts of some secret Catholics, he was converted back to the Catholic faith and decided to become a priest. Since this was impossible in England, he went to the English seminary in Douay, France, where he was ordained in 1579. He smuggled himself back into England and began his ministry to hidden Catholics. After two years he was finally trapped by Elizabeth's police in a house in London. He was imprisoned in the Tower of London, where he was tortured to make him reveal what he knew about other priests in England. Despite having needles thrust under his fingernails and being racked to the limit on two successive days, he revealed nothing. After a public trial, he was taken to Tyburn Hill, where he was hanged, drawn, and quartered. The date of his death is December 1, 1582. He was canonized in 1970 as one of the forty new English and Welsh saints.

Other saints with this name:

St. Alexander (Constantinople) *Aug. 28*
St. Alexander (Egypt) *Feb. 26*
St. Alexander (Jerusalem) *Mar. 18*

# Alexis (*Greek:* Helper)    July 17

**Other Forms: Alex, Alexei, Sasha**

St. Alexis was the son of a Roman senator. Pledging himself to God, he fled his home rather than be forced into a marriage. He made his way to Asia Minor, where he lived as a hermit and busied himself with good works. Because of his holiness, people were attracted to him. This caused him to flee again. He eventually returned to Rome and found shelter in a shed on his father's estate without anyone knowing who he was. He spent his time in prayer and supported himself by begging. After his death, papers found on his body revealed his identity. It is said that both the Pope and Emperor attended his funeral in 404. He was declared a saint because of the many miracles wrought in his name.

15

# Aloysius  *(Latin* for Louis [see])  June 21

Aloysius Gonzaga was born into a noble Italian family in 1568. His father destined him for a military career and, when the boy was only four years old, dressed him as a soldier and made him mix with troops he was organizing for the king of Spain. Aloysius learned some dirty words from the soldiers and used them, a fact he was to regret for the rest of his life. He called this period his life of sin. When he was seven he decided to devote himself to God and at age eleven made a vow of perpetual chastity. His father forced him to serve at various royal courts, refusing to let him follow a religious vocation. When he was 17, he entered the Society of Jesus where he quickly won a reputation for innocence and sanctity. He died when he was but 23 years old. He is a patron of youth.

# Alphonse  *(Teutonic:* Eager for Battle)

(The two best known saints with this name are listed under the Latin form, Alphonsus.)

### Other Forms: Alfonso, Alonzo, Lon

ALPHONSUS LIGUORI  (Aug. 1)

St. Alphonsus Liguori was born into a pious family in Naples, Italy, in 1696. Of nine children in the family, three boys became priests and two girls became nuns. Alphonsus did not plan to become a priest. A brilliant student, he graduated with a law degree when only sixteen years old. His legal skills were much in demand, and his career prospered. When he was 27 years old, he lost a case and felt so bad about it that he began to look into the values of his life. He decided that he should use his talents solely for God and thus became a priest. He first worked among the poor in the countryside around Naples but realized that there was so much to be done that he needed help. He founded the Redemptorist Congregation, which spread rapidly and not too long after his death even reached America. St. Alphonsus became a bishop but later resigned to live in his congregation. He was more than ninety years old when he died. One of the miracles put forward for his canonization was his ability to be in two places at once. On September 21, 1774, when he was in his bishopric of Sant' Agata de Goti, he also appeared in Rome to comfort the dying Pope Clement XIV. He is the patron of confessors.

Another saint with this name:

St. Alphonsus Rodriguez, S.J. (Spain) *Oct. 30*

# Ambrose (*Greek:* Immortal)　　　　　　　　　　Dec. 7

St. Ambrose is thought to have been born in Trier, Germany, where his father was prefect of Gaul. He himself entered the service of the Roman Empire and eventually became governor of a province centered in Milan, Italy. While he was ruling there, the bishop died. The people could not agree who should be the new bishop until someone proposed Ambrose's name and he was immediately elected. Because Ambrose was only studying to be a Christian, within a few days he was baptized and ordained a priest and bishop. The young nobleman became the advisor to three Roman emperors. He was known for his brilliance in preaching. A young African, Augustine of Hippo, heard him preach one day, was converted to the Catholic Church, and became the famous St. Augustine. Saint Ambrose wrote many theological works, and some of his hymns are still sung in church today. He died in 397. He is the protector of bees and domestic animals.

Other saints with this name:

St. Ambrose Barlow (England) *Oct. 25*
St. Ambrose Kibuuke (Uganda) *June 3*


# Amos (*Hebrew:* Brave)　　　　　　　　　　Mar. 31

Amos was one of the twelve minor prophets of the Old Testament. He lived in Judah, near Bethlehem, and describes himself, in the book of the Bible that bears his name, as a herdsman and as one who cares for trees. He was called by God to preach repentance to the Northern Kingdom. He went to both Bethel and Samaria preaching against the moral conditions that he found. His prophetic mission lasted about a year, after which he returned home.


# Andrew (*Greek:* Manly)　　　　　　　　　　Nov. 30

### Other forms: André, Andreas, Andres, Drew

Andrew belonged to a family of fishermen who had their business at Capernaum on the Sea of Galilee. Andrew was also a disciple of John the Baptist and was with John at the Jordan River when Jesus Christ came to be baptized. Hearing John praise Jesus, Andrew sought Him out and stayed with Him for a time. He also introduced Jesus to his brother, Simon Peter. When it came time for Jesus to form His band of Apostles, He

*ST. ANDREW*

18

went to Capernaum and selected Andrew and Simon Peter as His first Apostles. Andrew remained close to Jesus and an important member of the apostolic band. At the time when 5,000 people were with Jesus with nothing to eat, it was Andrew who told Jesus about the boy with a few loaves of bread and some fish, which Jesus multiplied to feed the crowd. Another time when some people wanted to see Jesus, it was Andrew who arranged the meeting. Tradition says that Andrew preached the Gospel around the Black Sea, where he was martyred on a cross in the shape of an X. He is the patron of fishermen, fish dealers, and women who wish to become mothers.

Other saints by this name:

St. Andrew Avellino (Italy) *Nov. 10*
St. Andrew Bobola (Poland) *May 16*
St. Andrew Corsini (Italy) *Feb. 4*
St. Andrew Fournet (France) *May 13*
St. Andrew Kaqqwa (Uganda) *June 3*

# Angelo *(Italian:* Angel) May 5

### Another Form: Angel

Saint Angelo was born in Jerusalem of Jewish parents who had been converted to Christianity. He and his brother became Carmelite monks. For five years he lived as a hermit on Mount Carmel, and then he went to Sicily to preach the Gospel. He converted many Jews. In the course of his preaching, he denounced a wealthy and powerful man who led a very evil life. One day in 1220, when St. Angelo was preaching to a crowd of Sicilians, this man and some followers broke through the crowd and stabbed St. Angelo to death. As he lay dying, he prayed for the people of Sicily and forgave his murderer.

# Anselm *(Teutonic:* Divine Helmet) Apr. 21

### Another Form: Ansel

St. Anselm was born in northern Italy about 1033. His family was prominent and had royal connections. As a boy Anselm wanted to be a priest, but his father would not allow this. Instead his father introduced him to court life and the young man enjoyed the pleasures of easy living. After the death of his mother, Anselm and his father quarreled. Anselm left home and made his way to France. For several years he drifted without purpose before the idea of the priesthood returned to him. He entered the Abbey of Bec in Normandy and became a monk. He quickly won a reputation throughout Europe for his learning and holiness. He became the abbot of his monastery and had to go frequently to England on business. During one trip, King William Rufus of England asked him to become Bishop of Canterbury, and he remained in this post until his death in 1109. Because of his writings on philosophy and theology and the many prayers he composed, St. Anselm is ranked as a Doctor (Teacher) of the Church.

# Anthony (*Greek:* Priceless)

## Other Forms: Antoine, Anton, Antonio, Antony

ST. ANTHONY OF EGYPT                                        (Jan. 17)

Anthony was born in Upper Egypt about 250. When he was twenty, his parents died leaving him with much property and wealth. After providing for his sister, he gave away all his money and went into the desert as a hermit. Despite his wish to be alone with God, people came to him with their troubles, and he is said to have worked miraculous cures for them. Disciples also sought him out, and he founded two monasteries. He died at the age of 105 in the cave that was his last home. St. Anthony is called the "father of monasticism."

ST. ANTHONY OF PADUA                                       (June 13)

Born in Lisbon, Portugal, in 1195, St. Anthony was twenty-five years old when the bodies of the first Franciscan martyrs were brought back from Africa for burial. He was so impressed by the sacrifice of these men that he joined the Franciscans and set out for Africa in the hope of finding martyrdom. He became sick, however, and had to return home. On the way back to Europe a storm forced his boat to Sicily. Here he joined some other Franciscans going to their headquarters in Italy. No one there expected him and he was left pretty much on his own. He lived in a cave near a monastery in Forli, coming out only for prayers and to sweep the monastery. One day a monk who was to preach to the community failed to appear and some of the members, probably as a joke, asked the young sweeper to take his place. Without any preparation Anthony gave a sermon that revealed both his theological knowledge and preaching skill. From that day on, he spent his life preaching throughout Italy, France and Belgium. It is said that in imitation of St. Francis he one day preached to fish which came to the surface of the water to hear his sermon. He was very famous when he died at the age of thirty-six in Padua, Italy. St. Anthony is a Doctor of the Church and is prayed to for the protection of horses and to find lost objects.

*ST. ANTHONY OF PADUA*

Born in Normandy, France, in 1601, St. Anthony Daniel was studying law when he decided to become a Jesuit. After training, he was sent to
Canada to work among the Huron Indians. On July 4, 1648, he was just
finishing Mass at St. Joseph's Mission when the village was raided by Iroquois Indians. Dipping his handkerchief in water, he baptized as many
catechumens as he could, urging the Christians to flee to safety. He then
went out to meet the Iroquois, hoping to gain more time for his Christians
to escape. The invaders showered him with arrows. The Iroquois dragged
his body into the church, which was then set on fire.

Other saints with this name:

St. Anthony Claret (Spain) *Oct. 24*
St. Anthony Zaccaria (Italy) *July 5*

# Arnold (*Teutonic:* Strength of an Eagle)            July 8

### Other Forms: Arnaldo, Arnoldo

St. Arnold was a Greek by birth who became a member of the court of
the Emperor Charlemagne. He led a very holy life and was called a "model of Christian virtue." He was also known for his devotion to the poor. He
died shortly after the year 800, and a village in France still bears his
name.

# Augustine (Diminutive of Augustus,            Aug. 28
*Latin:* Majestic)

### Other Forms: Agostino, August, Augustin, Austin

St. Augustine was born in North Africa in 354. His father, Patrick,
was a pagan who was baptized on his deathbed. His mother was St.
Monica. Monica instructed her son in Christianity but he had no interest
in religion. From the time he was sixteen he led a sensual life, took up
with a woman by whom he had a son, Adeodatus. A brilliant teacher, Augustine first taught in Carthage and then went to Italy to teach in Milan.
He heard a sermon by St. Ambrose and was so moved that he went to him,
began restudying Christianity and was finally baptized by Ambrose along
with Adeodatus. During all these years, Monica had been praying for his
conversion. After the death of St. Monica, who had accompanied him to
Italy, Augustine returned to Africa. He sold his estates, gave the money to
the poor, and began studies for the priesthood. After he was ordained he

was assigned to a church in Hippo where he gained fame as a preacher. In 396 he became Bishop of Hippo and spent the next thirty-five years preaching, writing and governing his diocese. He died on August 28, 430, while the Vandals were storming Hippo during the fall of the Roman Empire. He was one of the Church's greatest theologians, and almost a hundred of his books and over two hundred letters have survived. Also, more than four hundred of his sermons have been preserved. He is a Doctor of the Church.

Other saints with this name:

St. Augustine of Canterbury (England) *May 28*
St. Augustine Webster (England) *May 4*
Bl. Augustine Chapdelaine (Vietnam) *Feb. 28*

# Barnabas (*Hebrew:* Son of Consolation) June 11

### Another Form: Barnaby

Barnabas was a Jew of the tribe of Levi, a native of the island of Cyprus. He was in Jerusalem about the time of the first Pentecost, was converted, sold a field and placed the money at the feet of the Apostles to be used for the Christian community. He was a friend of St. Paul, making missionary journeys with him. He also traveled to preach the Gospel with John Mark. He took part in the Council of Jerusalem. Tradition says that he was stoned to death in Salamis by Jews from Syria.

# Bartholomew (*Hebrew:* Son of Talmai) Aug. 24

### Other Forms: Bart, Bartel, Bartolommeo, Barry

Bartholomew is listed in the Gospels and Acts as one of the Twelve Apostles. His name is always linked to that of Philip, who is thought to have been a close friend. He is also believed to be the one who is sometimes called Nathaniel. He was brought to Jesus by Philip and from that time on followed the Lord. He was present when Jesus appeared on the shore of the Sea of Galilee to eat bread and fish with His disciples. Tradition says that he preached the Gospel "in nearer India." He is the patron of butchers, tanners and bookbinders.

*ST. ANTHONY OF EGYPT*

24

# Basil (*Greek:* Royal)                                              Jan. 2

### Other Forms: Vasily, Vassily

St. Basil the Great is honored as a Doctor (Teacher) of the Church in both the Greek and Latin Churches. He was one of the great figures of early Christianity. He is considered, along with St. Gregory Nazianzen, as the greatest of the Greek Fathers. He was born in 330 of Christian parents in Asia Minor. Early in life he desired to lead an ascetic life given to study and writing. He resisted Arianism and wrote much against the heresy. Because of his wisdom and holiness, he was made Bishop of Caesarea in 370. He wrote a monastic rule which is still followed today in the Eastern Churches, being to the East what St. Benedict's rule was to the West. Worn out by work and penances, he died at 49 years of age, January 1, 379.


# Bede (*Celtic:* Life)                                               May 27

One writer has called St. Bede "the brightest ornament of the English nation." He was born in Northumbria in 673. He entered the monastery at Jarrow and was educated there, becoming a priest. He was a master of Latin and Greek, and his writings show his interest in many different subjects. He wrote a history of the English Church which is a most valuable record and because of which he is called "Father of English Historians." He was the foremost scholar and teacher of his time. He died on the eve of the Ascension (735), and his last words were "Glory be to the Father and the Son and the Holy Spirit." He was buried with great honor in Durham Cathedral. He has been named Doctor (Teacher) of the Church.


# Benedict (*Latin:* Blessing)                                        July 11

### Other Forms: Benoit, Bennett, Benito

St. Benedict, the father of modern monasticism and founder of the Benedictine Order, is one of the great figures of the Church. He was born in Umbria in what is now Italy. As a youth he went to Rome to study, but seeing the sinful habits of his fellow students and fearing he himself might be led into sin, he fled into the mountains around Subiaco, where he lived in a cave. Although he was removed from the world, his reputation for holiness and his wisdom caused others to go to him for spiritual direction. Gradually a small band of monks formed about him. One day, Benedict and his followers left Subiaco and went to Monte Cassino, where there was a sacred grove of trees with altars to Apollo, Jupiter, and Venus. Benedict smashed the altars and set the grove on fire to destroy the last remains of paganism. He and his companions built a monastery there which has grown and grown over the centuries. Benedict drew up a rule for his community which had for its motto "to work is to pray." His monasteries spread throughout Europe, and many cities grew up around them. He died in 543. Pope Pius XII called St. Benedict "The Father of Europe." He is prayed to against kidney disease and temptations of the devil.

Other saints with this name:

St. Benedict Joseph Labre (France) *Apr. 16*
St. Benedict the Black (Italy) *Apr. 4*


# Benjamin (*Hebrew:* Son of the Right Hand)    Mar. 31

### Another Form: Benson

Benjamin is an ancient name appearing first in the story of Joseph in Egypt in the Book of Genesis. Benjamin was Joseph's youngest brother, the son of the patriarch Jacob. The saint with this name lived in Persia and was a deacon who preached Christianity. The pagan king ordered Benjamin to stop his preaching against the magi and fire worshippers of Persia. Benjamin refused to do so, and the king had him arrested. Despite many tortures to get him to deny his faith, Benjamin remained firm in his trust in God. Furious at his failure, the king ordered Benjamin executed (about 420 A.D.).


# Bernard (*German:* Bold as a Bear)    May 28

### Other Forms: Barnard, Bernadino, Bernardo, Bernhard, Nardo

St. Bernard of Menthon was the founder of two famous Swiss hospices that saved the lives of many travelers. French and German pilgrims on the way to Rome crossed into Italy over two Alpine passes that were subject to unseasonal snowstorms. Many pilgrims caught in such storms became lost in snowdrifts and froze to death. To help these pilgrims, St. Bernard founded a hospice on each of the two main passes which became known as Great and Little St. Bernard. Monks were trained to seek pilgrims lost in the storm and bring them to safety and shelter in the hospices. A special breed of dog was developed to aid in this work, and this dog is today our huge St. Bernard dog. St. Bernard died in 1081. Pope Pius XI named him patron of mountain climbers.

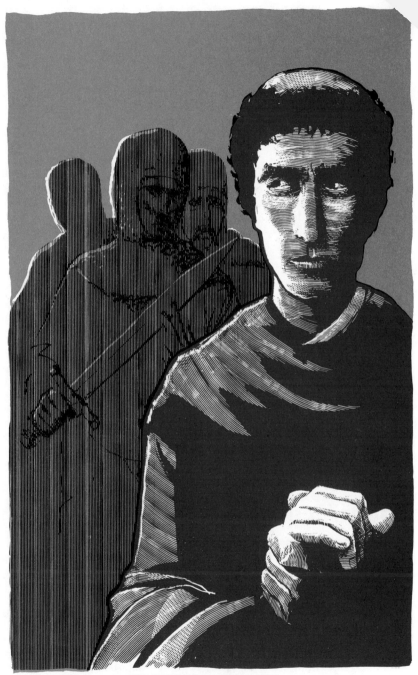

*ST. THOMAS BECKET*

# Blase (*Latin:* Babbler) Feb. 3

### Another Form: Blaise

St. Blase was the Bishop of Sebaste in Armenia. He once saved a boy from choking to death and for this reason is invoked against diseases of the throat. He was arrested under Licinius for being the chief of the Christians. He was tortured and beheaded in Sebaste in 316. His feast became popular in Asia Minor and was brought to Europe by the Crusaders. On his feast day throats are blessed, seeking the intercession of St. Blase.

# Bonaventure (*Latin:* Good Attempt) July 15

St. Bonaventure is popularly known as the Seraphic Doctor. He was born in Italy in 1231. At the age of twenty, he entered the Franciscan Order. After he was ordained a priest, he became a teacher. Along with St. Thomas Aquinas, he was a professor at the University of Paris. He was later elected Superior General of the Franciscans, and when his term was up, Pope Gregory X named him a cardinal and Bishop of Albano. He died in 1274 during the Council of Lyons. He wrote many books of scholarship and also a popular life of St. Francis. Because of his learning and writings, he was named a Doctor (Teacher) of the Church.

# Boniface (*Latin:* Doer of Good Things) June 5

Although known as the Apostle of Germany, Boniface was born in England about 680. He entered the abbey at Exeter as a boy and for some years taught other monks. His dream was to convert Germany. He finally received permission to go to Rome and propose a mission to Germany. Pope Gregory II received him kindly, commissioned him as a missioner to Germany, made him a bishop, and changed his name from Winifrid to Boniface. Arriving in Germany, Boniface went directly to the center of pagan worship. The Germans believed that their god, Thor, resided in a sacred oak tree. Boniface chopped the tree down and began to preach Christianity. Boniface erected bishoprics, founded monasteries and churches, bringing many missioners from England to teach the Germans.

*ST. BONIFACE*

In 755, at the age of 75, while on a mission journey, his band was attacked by pagans, and he was killed by a blow to the head. He was buried at the monastery in Fulda which he founded and where his relics can be seen today.

# Brendan (*Celtic:* Sword)                    May 16

### Other Forms: Brandon, Brennan

St. Brendan was born in County Kerry, Ireland. He built several churches in that area. He founded a monastery at Clonfert and made many journeys, particularly to Britain. A book appearing after his death, called *Navigatio*, and supposedly written by him, tells of some of these journeys, which Brendan made in a leather boat. Students of the book claim that it shows Brendan reached Iceland and America. It is said that Columbus was familiar with the book and that it inspired him to seek the land discovered by St. Brendan. The book also tells about the monks who followed St. Brendan and lived his rule of life. He died at Clonfert about 580.

# Brian (*Celtic:* Strong)                    Dec. 10

### Other Forms: Bryan, Bryant

Bl. Brian Lacey was one of the Catholic martyrs put to death by the English in London in 1591. He is described as "a gentleman from Yorkshire." He was betrayed to the authorities by his own brother for aiding an underground priest, Father Montford Scott. He was tortured, and when he refused to deny the Catholic religion, he was sentenced to death. He was executed at Tyburn Prison on Dec. 10, 1591.

# Brice (*Anglo Saxon:* Breach)                    Nov. 13

### Other Form: Bruce

St. Brice was an orphan who was rescued as a child by St. Martin of Tours. Growing up, he was proud, ungrateful, and a great trial to St. Martin, who was often urged to send him packing. St. Martin refused saying that God's grace would change Brice. St. Martin was right. Brice changed, became a bishop, had many trials but remained faithful to God. He is the patron for those who suffer stomach disorders. He died in 444.

*ST. BENEDICT*

31

# Bruno (*Teutonic:* Brown)                                    Oct. 6

St. Bruno was born into a noble family in Cologne, Germany, about 1035. He was a brilliant student and soon became one of the foremost theologians of his day. One of his students was the future Pope Urban II. He was in line to become a bishop, but worldly honors meant nothing to him. With some friends he retired to a remote area and founded the Carthusian Order. Pope Urban II called him to Rome as an advisor. Bruno obeyed and went but was not happy at the papal court. The Pope, in an attempt to keep him, offered to make him an archbishop. Bruno declined and the Pope allowed him to go to Calabria and begin a new Carthusian monastery. Here he died a holy death in 1101.

Other saints with this name:

Bruno Serinkuma (Uganda) *June 3*
Bruno of Wurtzburg (Germany) *May 27*


# Camillus (*Latin:* Temple Servant)                          July 14

### Another Form: Camille, Camillo

St. Camillus de Lellis was born in southern Italy in 1550. After some years of worldly life, he decided to devote himself to the sick. He became a priest, gathered some followers, and founded a religious order whose members were pledged to care for the sick. He died in 1614.


# Casimir (*Slavic:* Peaceful)                                 Mar. 4

### Other Forms: Cass, Casper

Casimir was the third child born to King Casimir III of Poland. His birthday is Oct. 5, 1458. From an early age he was given to prayer and desired nothing more than to become a saint. The young prince slept on the floor, rather than in his comfortable bed, wore a hair shirt, and practiced many penances. Prince Casimir was offered the crown of Hungary but turned it down because he felt it belonged to another. He governed Poland from 1481 to 1483 while his father was away in Lithuania. During this time an attempt was made to have him marry the daughter of the Emperor of Germany. He refused because he had privately made a vow of virginity. He died in his 24th year, on March 5, 1484. He is known for his devotion to the Eucharist and the Virgin Mary. He was buried with his favorite hymn to Mary in his hands.

# Chad *(Celtic:* Martial)  Mar. 2

Chad was a monk in a monastery in Ireland before being appointed abbot of a monastery at Lastingham, England. Shortly afterwards, the bishop of the area died, and Chad was selected to succeed him. Later he was transferred to be Bishop of Litchfield. He had a great love for the poor and spent much time among them. When the archbishop told him that he should travel about his diocese on horseback, Chad replied that he wished to imitate the Apostles by going about on foot. He died, a victim of plague, in 672.

# Charles *(Teutonic:* Strong)  Nov. 4

**Other Forms: Carl, Carlo, Carlos, Carroll, Cary, Karl, Karol**

When he was born Oct. 2, 1538, into a wealthy Italian family, Charles Borromeo had everything against him for becoming a saint. He attended the best schools, and his personable manner made him popular among the rich and powerful. His uncle became Pope Pius IV and almost immediately made Charles, then only 22, a cardinal and Archbishop of Milan. He took up residence at the Roman court, where he had much influence in the Council of Trent. His brother's death in 1562 deeply affected him. Although he led a good life, he now began to lead a holy one. He was ordained a priest, returned to his archdiocese, and set about reforming it. He used his own money to found seminaries, schools, and hospitals. During a great plague he went about the streets aiding the dying. He fasted on bread and water, slept on the ground, and gave his fortune away to the poor. He died when only 46, and his last words were, "Behold, I come."

Other saints with this name:

St. Charles Lwanga (Uganda) *June 3*
St. Charles Garnier (Canada) *Sept. 26*

# Christian *(Latin:* Belonging to Christ)  June 12

St. Christian was an Irish bishop, brother of St. Malachy of Armagh. He was made Bishop of Clogher in 1126. He led a holy life and was devoted to the care of the people of his diocese. He died in 1138.

*ST. CHRISTOPHER*

# Christopher (*Greek:* Christ-bearer)                    July 25

### Other Forms: Christophe, Cristobal, Cristoforo

St. Christopher was one of the most popular saints in the Middle Ages, and devotion to him continues to this day. He is said to have lived about 250. In the Greek Church he is honored as one martyred in Lycia during the persecution of Christianity by Decius. There are many legends of him in the Latin Church. The chief one is that he became a ferryman who helped people across a turbulent river. He did this as a charitable work for Christ. One night he was hailed by a child, and as he carried the little boy across the stream, he learned he was carrying the Christ Child. St. Christopher is the patron of travelers, fruit dealers and archers. His aid is invoked against sudden death and storms.

Other saints with this name:

St. Christopher of Cordova (Spain) *Aug. 20*
St. Christopher Buxton (England) *Oct. 1*


# Clair (*Latin:* Clear)                    Nov. 4
### Other Forms: Clare, Clarus

St. Clair was an Englishman of noble birth who was born at Rochester. He became a priest and went to France to live in a hermitage. There he was murdered for his resistance to sin. The dates of his life are uncertain, about the eighth century.


# Clarence (*Latin:* Illustrious)                    Apr. 26

Very little is known of St. Clarence other than that he succeeded St. Aetherius as Bishop of Vienne (France). He died about 620.


# Claude (*Latin:* Lame)                    Mar. 10

### Another Form: Claudius

St. Claude was a member of a Roman legion stationed in Sebaste in Asia Minor. During the persecution of the Emperor Licinius, forty members of this legion were put to death when they refused to sacrifice to the

Roman gods, because they were Christians. Claude and his companions were stripped and left naked overnight on a frozen lake. The next morning their legs were broken, and they were cremated.

Other saints with this name:

St. Claude of Besancon (France) *June 6*
St. Claude of Vienna (Austria) *June 1*
St. Claude of Rome (Italy) *Dec. 3*

# Clement *(Latin:* Merciful)                    Nov. 23

Clement was the third Pope after St. Peter to rule the Church. Some think he was Jewish, others a Roman. The basilica named after him in Rome is said to have been built over his house, where St. Peter often stayed. He wrote a famous letter to the Corinthians which is one of the most important documents of early Church history because it showed the importance of the papacy even at the end of the first century. The Church honors him as a martyr. He is the patron of boatmen and prayed to for sick children.

Other saints with this name:

St. Clement of Rome (Italy) *Nov. 21*
St. Clement Mary Hofbauer (Austria) *Mar. 15*
St. Clementius (Greece) *Nov. 14*

# Colman *(Irish:* Short for Columba or Columban)    July 8

There are well over a hundred Irish saints named Colman. One of the best known was a missioner who left Ireland to preach the Gospel to the German tribes of Thuringia. Along with his companion missioners, Kilian and Tonan, he was martyred there for his labors about 690.

Other saints with this name:

St. Colman of Cloine (Ireland) *Nov. 26*
St. Colman of Dromore (Ireland) *June 7*
St. Colman of Lindisfarne (Ireland) *Feb. 18*

# Columba *(Gaelic* from *Latin:* Dove)

**Other Forms: Columban, Columbanus, Columcille, Col-
man, Colum, Colin, Cullen**

ST. COLUMBAN                                             (Nov. 23)

St. Columban was born in Ireland about 540. He took his early training in the monastery at Bangor under St. Congall. Because of his learning,
he was invited by the King of Burgundy (France) to preach the Gospel
there. He took twelve monks and landed in France in 590. He founded
many monasteries but the one at Luxeuil had the greatest influence,
educating many bishops and missioners. He had great influence throughout Europe, and among the many reforms he introduced was the Irish
practice of private confession. He founded his last monastery at Bobbio in
Italy and died there the following year.

ST. COLUMBA                                              (June 9)

While there are a number of saints by this name, the one best known
is St. Columba of Iona. Like Columban, he was Irish and a great figure of
Western monasticism. He founded a hundred monasteries and spent the
last 34 years of his life as a missioner in Scotland, dying there in 597 at the
monastery of Iona which he had begun.

# Constantine *(Latin:* Firm)                          Mar. 11

St. Constantine was a Cornish prince who gave up his crown to become a monk. He founded a monastery at Govan on the Clyde River and
worked to convert the area. He gave his life for the Faith in 576.

# Cormac *(Celtic:* Charioteer)                        Sept. 14

St. Cormac is listed as the first Bishop of Cashel (Ireland). He put together the famous Cashel Psalter, a book of psalms. He was also King of
Munster and died in battle in 908.

# Cornelius *(Latin:* Horn)

### Other Forms: Connor, Conor, Cornel, Neal, Neil

ST. CORNELIUS, POPE                                           (Sept. 16)

Cornelius was ordained Bishop of Rome and made pope in 251. He had to oppose enemies both within and outside the Church. He was sent into exile by the Emperor Gallus and died in 253 after a short reign as pope. His body was taken back to Rome and buried in the catacomb of St. Callistus. Because of his sufferings, the Church considers him a martyr. His name is listed in the first Eucharistic Prayer (the Roman Canon).

ST. CORNELIUS THE CENTURION                                   (Feb. 2)

Cornelius was a Roman officer, a centurion, who was in charge of the Italian Cohort stationed at Caesarea in the Holy Land. Some think he may have been the same centurion whose servant was healed by Jesus, who had helped build the synagogue at Capernaum. At any event, the Acts of the Apostles tells us that he had a vision which instructed him to send to Joppa for Simon Peter. St. Peter came, taught Cornelius about Jesus. He baptized Cornelius, his family, and some of his friends. The incident is important in Church history because it was the first baptisms of Gentiles by Peter. You can read the story in Chapter 10 of the Acts of the Apostles.

# Cyril *(Greek:* Lordly)

### Other Forms: Cyr, Kyril

ST. CYRIL OF JERUSALEM                                        (Mar. 18)

St. Cyril of Jerusalem is one of the Fathers and Teachers of the Church. He was born in Palestine and became Bishop of Jerusalem about 350. He had a difficult life, being driven from his bishopric by Arian heretics and emperors who favored the heresy in an attempt to divide the Church. He wrote a catechism which has come down to us that he used to prepare new Christians for baptism. He died about 387.

ST. CYRIL OF ALEXANDRIA                                       (June 27)

St. Cyril of Alexandria was also a Teacher (Doctor) of the Church. He was born in Egypt in 370. He entered a monastery, became a priest, and finally Bishop of Alexandria. He too had to fight against heretics. He was a leader at the Council of Ephesus. He wrote many books to defend the Church. He was one of the earliest to defend the truth that Mary is the Mother of God. He died in 444.

*DAVID*

39

# Damian (*Greek:* Tamer)

### Other Forms: Damiano, Damien, Damon

St. Damian with his brother, St. Cosmas, went from Arabia to Syria to practice medicine. They followed the Gospel command to give freely of their gifts. As a result of their medical mission, they won many converts. Because of this, they came to the attention of Lysias, who had been ordered by the emperor to hunt out Christians. Lysias had them arrested and ordered them to sacrifice to the Roman gods. When they refused, he had them tortured, and when they still would not worship the pagan gods, he had them beheaded. They were buried at Cyr in Syria, and later a great church was built there in their honor. Many years later, when the Emperor Justinian was very sick, he prayed to Sts. Damian and Cosmas for a cure. When his prayer was answered, he enlarged the town of Cyr and built a new church to the martyrs. As a result, devotion to them spread throughout the empire. Their names are listed in the First Eucharistic Prayer (the Roman Canon) among the martyrs to whom the whole Church prays. They died about 300. St. Cosmas is patron of doctors and druggists.


# Daniel (*Hebrew:* The Lord Is Judge)

### Other Forms: Dan, Niel

DANIEL (July 21)

Daniel was one of the great prophets of the Old Testament. When he was a youth, the King of Babylon attacked Jerusalem, overran it, and took many of its people into captivity, among them Daniel. Because he was handsome and bright, he was trained in the king's household, where he remained faithful to Jewish law despite many temptations. He became very popular with the king, for whom he interpreted dreams, including the fall of the kingdom to invaders. Under the conquering King Darius, Daniel was thrown into a cage of lions to be eaten alive, but when God saved his life, Darius the king, ruled that all in his kingdom were free to worship Daniel's God. You can read all about Daniel in the Book of Daniel in the Old Testament.

ST. DANIEL OF MURANO (Mar. 31)

St. Daniel of Murano was born in Germany. He went to Venice, Italy, where he became a successful trader. A very holy man, he gave his profits to the poor and lived in a monastery in Murano. He was murdered by robbers in 1411.

# David *(Hebrew:* Beloved)  Dec. 29

David was born in Bethlehem about a thousand years before Christ. At that time Saul was King of Israel but he had lost the favor of God because of disobedience. Therefore, under the inspiration of God, the Prophet Samuel went to Bethlehem and anointed the boy David. At that time, Israel was at war with the Philistines. One day his father sent David with food to his brothers who were in Saul's army. When David arrived in the camp, he found the Israelites fearful because the Philistines had a giant of a warrior against whom no man could stand. In fact, the giant whose name was Goliath only had to show himself and the Israelites fled. David told King Saul that he would meet Goliath. "You are only a boy," the king told him. "I have killed a lion and a bear that attacked my father's sheep," David replied. "The Lord will deliver me out of the hands of this Philistine." David went to meet Goliath with only a slingshot because the armor given him was too big and the sword too heavy. The giant came at the boy with sword upraised but David took his slingshot and hit Goliath between the eyes with a stone, knocking him to the ground. He took Goliath's sword and cut off the giant's head. David was made a member of the king's household because of his bravery, and he entertained Saul by playing the harp. Later when Saul died in battle, Samuel anointed David as king. As king, David made Jerusalem his capital. He brought the Ark of the Covenant there. He wrote beautiful psalms (songs) to God which can be found in the Bible's Book of Psalms. David's own story can be read in the First and Second Book of Samuel. David's son Solomon succeeded his father to the throne and built the first great Temple to God. Solomon like his father was a great and wise king.

Other saints with this name:

St. David the Hermit (Mesopotamia) *June 26*
St. David of Russia *July 24*
St. David of Scotland *May 24*
St. David of Wales *Mar. 1*


# Denis *(Greek:* God of Nyassa)

## Other Forms: Dennis, Dion, Dionysius, Sidney, Sydney

ST. DENIS  (Oct. 9)

St. Denis, bishop and martyr, is the patron saint of France. According to St. Martin of Tours, Denis was made the head of a mission band and sent from Rome to Gaul to preach the Gospel. He worked in the district of the present Paris and is considered to be the first bishop of that city. Because of his missionary work, Denis, along with two companions, was put to death there about the year 250.

41

*ST. DOMINIC*

St. Paul arrived in Athens about the year 50 A.D. He preached the Gospel in the synagogue there without much success and also appeared in the marketplace to talk about Jesus. Athens at this time was full of idols of gods from everywhere. Some philosophers invited Paul to the Areopagus to speak to them, and here he delivered his famous Sermon on the Unknown God (Acts of the Apostles 17:22-31). The sermon did not make many converts, but a few did join the Church. Among them was Denis the Areopagite. There is a tradition which says he became Bishop of Athens and later died a martyr. He is invoked against headaches.

# Dominic (*Latin:* I belong to the Lord)                    Aug. 8

### Other Forms: Domenico, Domingo, Dominick

St. Dominic de Guzman was born in Spain in 1170. He studied theology there, and after he became a priest he worked closely with the Bishop of Osma. In 1205, he and his bishop went to Rome where Pope Innocent III spoke to them about his concern over the Albigensian heresy. St. Dominic decided to work to convert these heretics. He gathered some followers, who were called "preachers," and sent them out barefoot and practicing penance to preach the true faith and to expose the mistakes of the Albigenses. Ten years later this group, which had grown rapidly, was approved as an order of the Church, the Order of Preachers (Dominicans). St. Dominic urged his followers to study "on journeys, at home, by day and night." Dominicans soon became the leading teachers in Europe. St. Dominic also founded a convent of women who were to become the Dominican Sisters. He died in Italy in 1221.

Other saints with this name:

St. Dominic Lorieatus (Italy) *Oct. 14*
St. Dominic Savio (Italy) *Mar. 9*

# Donald (*Celtic:* Dark Stranger)                    July 15

### Other Forms: Don, Donal

St. Donald lived in Forfar, Scotland, in the eighth century. Not very much is known about him other than that he was a husband and father who urged his family to love and serve God. His nine daughters all became nuns and formed their own small community.

# Edmund (*Old English:* Happy Protection)     Nov. 16

### Other Forms: Edmond, Eamon, Ned

St. Edmund was born into a very religious family at Abingdon, England. His mother wore a hairshirt and practiced strict penances. His father, Robert Rich, a successful merchant, entered a monastery. Edmund went to Europe to study and was in Paris teaching literature when he received word that his mother was dying. He returned home and after her death assumed responsibility for the family. He became a distinguished professor of sciences at Oxford University. After his sisters entered a convent, Edmund decided to become a priest. Following his ordination, he again became a professor at Oxford, this time teaching theology. He was appointed Archbishop of Canterbury, and his honesty and desire to protect the rights of the Church brought him the enmity of King Henry III. Other bishops and priests sided with the king against the archbishop. Finally, Edmund was forced to withdraw from England, going to France in 1240, where he died the same year.

Other saints with this name:

St. Edmund the King (England) *Nov. 20*
St. Edmund Campion (England) *Oct. 25*

# Edward (*Old English:* Rich Guardian)     Oct. 13

### Other Forms: Edoardo, Edouard, Eduard, Eduardo, Ned

St. Edward the Confessor was King of England for 23 years. He was born near Oxford about 1004. He succeeded to the throne of King Canute the Great, a Danish conqueror. Noted for his goodness and justice, Edward was a very popular king. He preferred to use wisdom rather than war to solve problems. He lowered taxes and made wise laws. He died January 5, 1066, and was succeeded by William the Conqueror.

Another saint by this name:

St. Edward the Martyr (England) *Mar. 18*

# Edwin (*Old English:* Rich Friend)     Oct. 12

St. Edwin was the King of Northumbria (England) who married St. Ethelburga. He was a pagan at the time of his wedding, but his wife's chaplain, St. Paulinus, converted him, and from then on he sought the conversion of his subjects. He fell in battle against a pagan king from Wales in 633.

# Elias *(Hebrew:* The Lord Is God) July 20

### Another Form: Elijah

St. Elias is a popular saint of the Eastern churches. He is one of the major prophets of the Old Testament who lived in the eighth century before Christ. His story is in the Book of Kings. Newer translations of the Bible refer to him as Elijah. According to the Second Book of Kings (Chapter 2), Elijah was taken up to heaven in a flaming chariot traveling in a whirlwind.

# Emil *(Latin:* Excelling) May 28

### Other Forms: Emile, Emilian, Emilion, Emilius, Emlyn

St. Emil was a Christian soldier stationed in Romania. Because he overthrew some pagan altars, he was arrested and buried alive at Drisna. He died in 362.

Other saints with this name:

St. Emilian of Nantes (France) *June 27*
St. Emilion (France) *Nov. 16*
St. Emilius of Capua (Italy) *Oct. 6*
St. Emil of Redon (France) *Oct. 11*

# Emmanuel *(Hebrew:* God With Us) Mar. 26

### Other Forms: Emanuel, Immanuel, Manolo, Manuel

Emmanuel is a name given to Jesus Christ. The Prophet Isaiah used it to refer to the expected Messiah. Most people who are given this name are so named in honor of Jesus. St. Emmanuel was a martyr under Diocletian in Asia Minor. Nothing else is known of him.

Another saint with this name:

Bl. Emmanuel Ruiz (Spain) *July 10*

# Eric (*Norse:* Ever-Ruler)                                    May 18

### Other Forms: Erik, Erich

St. Eric was elected King of Sweden in 1150. He led a holy life and was an inspiration to his people. His banner is held as a symbol of Swedish freedom, much as that of St. George in England. He died in battle in 1160 or 1161. This name is the Norse for Henry (*see*).


# Ernest (*Greek:* Serious)                                    Nov. 7

### Another Form: Ernesto

St. Ernest was a Benedictine abbot of South Germany. He joined one of the Crusades and remained behind to preach the Gospel in Palestine. He eventually made his way to Arabia where he was seized by Moslems and put to death at Mecca in 1148.


# Eugene (*Greek:* Well Born)                                    July 8

### Other Forms: Eugenio, Yevgeny

St. Eugene was the Bishop of Carthage in Africa at a time when the area was controlled by the Vandals, who favored the Arian heresy. Eugene's zeal and wisdom brought many Arians back into the Church. This alarmed the Arian bishops, and they appealed to King Huneric, who deported 5,000 Christians to the land of the Moors and forbade Eugene to act as bishop. Eugene was sent into exile where he remained until the death of Huneric. Under the new king, Eugene was allowed to return to Carthage and reopen the Catholic churches. However, when this king died, his successor, Aleric II, was an Arian and deported Eugene to France, where he died in 505.

Other saints with this name:

St. Eugene of Paris (France) *Nov. 15*
Pope St. Eugene (Italy) *June 2*


# Eustace (*Greek:* Fruitful)                                    Sept. 20

St. Eustace was a Roman officer who was a Christian. He, along with his wife and two sons, was arrested during the persecution of Hadrian (118 A.D.). Refusing to give up their faith, they were put to death. Their relics

*ST. FRANCIS OF ASSISI*

were kept in a church in Rome and later transferred to France where they were destroyed in 1567 by the anti-Catholic Huguenots.

# Fabian *(Latin:* Prosperous Farmer) Jan. 20

St. Fabian was still a layman when he was elected pope in 236. He was a great leader who reformed the discipline of the Church. He is said to have originated the Holy Thursday rite of Consecration of the Holy Oils which the Church still follows. He beautified the monuments to the martyrs. He was arrested during the persecution of Decian and put to death in 250.

# Felix *(Latin:* Happy) Nov. 20

### Other Forms: Felician, Felicio, Feliz

St. Felix was a hermit who for many years lived alone in a forest. One day a visitor came from Paris to see him. He was John of Matha, who was also to become a saint. John told Felix about a desire he had to work for the ransom of Christians who were being captured by Moslem pirates and taken across the Mediterranean Sea to Africa. Felix replied that he would also like to do this work. They decided that they would found a society in honor of the Blessed Trinity that would be devoted to the ransom of captives. Together they went to Rome to seek permission, which Pope Innocent III gave them. Thus the Trinitarian Order was born. They founded a monastery in Rome which John of Matha headed. St. Felix began another monastery in France which he governed until his death about 1212.

Other saints with this name:

St. Felix of Cordova (Spain) *July 27*
St. Felix of Metz (Germany) *Feb. 21*
St. Felix of Milan (Italy) *July 21*

# Ferdinand *(Teutonic:* Adventurous) May 30

### Other Forms: Fernando, Ferde, Fernand, Hernando

St. Ferdinand (Ferdinand III) was the King of Castile in Spain. His father was King of Leon and his mother the daughter of the King of Castile. After the death of her father in 1217, Ferdinand was proclaimed king of that country. When his own father died, Ferdinand also became King of Leon and thus united the two kingdoms. Moslems controlled a great part of Spain, and Ferdinand went to war with them. He drove the

Moslems out of Cordova, which they had held for five centuries, took back the kingdom of Murcia, and after a two-year siege entered Seville, one of Spain's most important cities. He thus began the end of Mohammedan control of Spain. He died in 1252.

# Fidelis (*Latin:* Faithful) · Apr. 24

**Another Form: Fidel**

St. Fidelis of Sigmaringen was born Mark Ray in southern Germany in 1577. He became a lawyer and was known for giving his services to the poor. In 1612 he entered the religious life by joining the Capuchin Fathers and taking the name by which he is now known. He was sent as a missioner to the Swiss Protestants. He made many converts but finally was stabbed to death by an armed gang on April 24, 1622.

# Francis (*Teutonic:* Free)

**Other Forms: Francesco, Francisco, Franco, Francois, Frank, Franz**

ST. FRANCIS OF ASSISI (Oct. 4)

St. Francis of Assisi is one of the most popular saints in the Roman calendar, loved by Catholics and non-Catholics because of the beauty of his life. He was born in Assisi, Italy, the son of a rich merchant. His early years were ones of delinquency, engaging in pleasures and brawls, and even spending time in the jails of Perugia. It was there that divine grace touched him and he was reborn as a saint. He took the Gospel counsels literally and began a life of poverty and love. Barefooted, in rough clothes, he begged for a living, preaching poverty, peace, and a love for all of God's creation. He called the wonders of nature and the animals his brothers and sisters. He worked with his hands, cared for lepers and the sick, swept out churches, built other churches with his own hands. Others attracted by his life joined him, and thus the Franciscan Order was born. Clare of Assisi sought him for spiritual guidance and under the inspiration of Francis she founded the Sisters of the Poor (Franciscan or Poor Clare Sisters). God gave a visible blessing to his work by bestowing on Francis the stigmata, or wounds of Christ. Worn out by his labors and difficulties caused by some of his followers, Francis lay down naked on the earth at the Portiuncula, a chapel he had built, and there welcomed his Sister Death on October 4, 1226. Pope Benedict XV called him the "most perfect image of Christ" that ever lived.

ST. FRANCIS XAVIER

## ST. FRANCIS XAVIER                                        (Dec. 3)

St. Francis Xavier is the patron of foreign missions. Born into a family of minor nobility which had its seat in the Castle of Xavier in the Basque country of Spain, Francis was privately tutored. Because of his brilliance, he was sent to the University of Paris, then the leading university in Europe. Here he gave himself up to pleasures as well as study. Another student at the university, a retired artillery captain named Ignatius Loyola, used to say to him, "Francis, what does it profit a man to gain the whole world if it costs him his soul?" Ignatius converted Francis to the service of Christ, and together with some other companions they formed the Society of Jesus. For some years, Francis worked in Italy, and then he was assigned to preach the Gospel in the Far East. He left for India in 1542. He had extraordinary success, baptizing tens of thousands. Fellow missioners told of his many miracles, even raising the dead to life. He also had the gift of tongues, people hearing him in their own languages. Later he worked in Japan, laying the foundations of Christianity there. He died on Sancian Island, alone and almost abandoned, in 1552, while trying to get into China which he could see in the distance. Francis' favorite prayer was, "Da mihi animas" (Give me souls). He was the greatest missioner the modern Church has ever produced.

## ST. FRANCIS DE SALES                                     (Jan. 24)

St. Francis de Sales was born in the Savoy area of France about 1566. His father wanted him to be a lawyer, so he became one, serving in the Senate of Savoy. However, his own wish was to become a priest, and this he did. He was very popular as a preacher and spiritual director. In 1603 he was appointed Bishop of Geneva. He inspired Madame de Chantal to found the Order of Visitation Sisters. Two of his books of spirituality, *Introduction to a Devout Life* and *Treatise on the Love of God,* have become classics, and he is the patron of writers. He died in 1622, calling himself "a useless servant."

Other saints with this name:

St. Francis Borgia (Spain) *Oct. 10*
St. Francis Caracciolo (Italy) *June 4*
St. Francis Solanus (Peru) *July 14*


# Frederick (*Teutonic:* Peace-Ruler)                      July 18

## Other Forms: Federico, Fred, Frederic, Friedrich

St. Frederick was a grandson of the King of the Frisians who grew up in holiness and became a priest. He was named Bishop of Utrecht (Holland) and worked to end paganism and idolatry in the region. He also reproved some members of the nobility for leading bad lives, thus making enemies. One of these enemies had him killed in 838 A.D.

# Gabriel *(Hebrew:* God's Strength)

## GABRIEL THE ARCHANGEL (Sept. 29)

Gabriel is one of the three angels who appear by name in the Bible. In the Book of Daniel, Gabriel appeared to the Prophet Daniel twice to explain a vision that the prophet had concerning the Messiah. In the New Testament Gabriel appears first to the priest Zachary (or Zechariah) while he is burning incense in the Temple. Gabriel tells him that Zachary's wife, Elizabeth, is to have a son whom he should name John. Gabriel identified himself this way: "I am Gabriel, who stands in the presence of God. I was sent to speak to you and bring you this good news." Six months later Gabriel appeared to the Virgin Mary, greeting her, "Hail, full of grace, the Lord is with you." Then Gabriel told her that she too was to have a son and that he should be named Jesus, about whose greatness he prophesied. You can read the account in the first chapter of the Gospel of Luke.

## ST. GABRIEL LALLEMAND (Oct. 19)

St. Gabriel Lallemand is a North American martyr. While preaching the Gospel in 1649 to the Huron Indians, he was captured by the Iroquois and put to death.

# George *(Greek:* Farmer) Apr. 23

**Other Forms: Georges, Giorgio, Igor, Jorge, Jurgen**

St. George suffered martyrdom in Palestine about the year 303. His popularity spread rapidly in both the Latin and Greek Churches. In England he received great devotion, and he became patron saint of that country, where his feast day was a holy day which the Archbishop of Canterbury ordered should have the same solemnity as Christmas. King Edward founded the Knights of St. George, which still exist as the Knights of the Garter. The most famous legend about St. George is how he went off on horseback in Libya and slew a terrible dragon that was devouring sheep and maidens, killing it with one blow of his lance. He is also patron of Boy Scouts.

Another saint with this name:

St. George of Cordova (Spain) *July 27*

# Gerald *(Teutonic:* Spear Rule) Mar. 13

### Other Forms: Geraldo, Garcia, Jerold

St. Gerald was an Irish monk who became the Abbot of Mayo. He led a very holy life, given to much prayer and fasting. He died about 722.

# Gerard *(Teutonic:* Strong Spear) Oct. 16

### Other Forms: Gerhard, Gerado, Girado, Girard

St. Gerard Majella was born in 1726, just south of Naples, Italy. As a boy he was made an apprentice to a tailor. He joined the newly founded Redemptorist Order as a lay brother. He was so holy that crowds followed him everywhere, trying to touch him and give him petitions. His superiors had to move him from monastery to monastery so that he would have some sort of normal religious life. He worked many miracles while alive. He died in 1755, still a young man. He is patron of mothers in difficult births.

Other saints with this name:

St. Gerard of Csanad (Hungary) *Sept. 24*
St. Gerard of Lunel (France) *May 25*

# Gervais *(Teutonic:* Spear Servant) June 15

### Other Forms: Gervas, Gervase, Gervasius, Jarvis, Jervis

On June 19, 386, St. Ambrose discovered the bodies of two martyrs who had been buried at Milan. They were named Gervase and Protasius. Devotion to the martyrs spread rapidly through the West, although little else was known about them.

# Gilbert *(Teutonic:* Bright Pledge) Feb. 4

St. Gilbert was born in England during the reign of William the Conqueror. He was the son of a Norman officer who had served the king so well that he had been awarded the Manor of Sempringham. Although his father wanted him to be a soldier, Gilbert chose to go to the University of

*ST. IGNATIUS LOYOLA*

Paris to study. Returning with his master of arts, he opened a school at Sempringham to serve poor children. The Bishop of Lincoln persuaded him to become a priest. After the death of his father, he used his inheritance to found two monasteries, one for nuns, the other for monks, called Gilbertines. Accused of helping the exiled Archbishop of Canterbury, St. Thomas of Becket, Gilbert was imprisoned for a time. He lived to be over a hundred and until his death in 1190 continued to serve the poor.

# Godfrey (*Teutonic:* God's Peace) Nov. 8

### Other Forms: Geoffrey, Goffredo, Gottfried, Jeff, Jeffrey

When St. Godfrey was a boy in France he entered the monastery of St. Quentin. There he was educated, became a monk, and was elected Abbot of Nogent. He became widely known for his wisdom and sanctity and was appointed Bishop of Amiens. He was never happy as bishop, always wishing to live as a simple monk. He died in 1115, loved and respected by the people he served.

# Gregory (*Greek:* Watchman)

### Other Forms: Gregor, Gregoire, Gregorio

GREGORY THE GREAT (Sept. 3)

Pope St. Gregory the Great is called a Doctor of the Church. He is also patron of singers and scholars. Born into a well-to-do family, Gregory entered public service and became Prefect (Governor) of Rome. Then he resigned his position of power, using his wealth to found the Monastery of St. Andrew, to which he withdrew. After being papal ambassador to Byzantium, he was elected pope in 590. As pope he set about reforming the Church. He revised the liturgy, encouraged the growth of monasticism, sent missioners to England and other European countries, established Gregorian chant music, revised the calendar, fought heresy, and developed the temporal powers of the papacy. He wrote many books on faith and morals. He died March 12, 604.

ST. GREGORY NAZIANZEN (Jan. 2)

A close friend and cooperator with St. Basil the Great in combatting Arianism and in developing monasticism, St. Gregory was born at Nazianzus in Asia Minor in 330. He became the Bishop of Constantinople and presided over the Second Ecumenical Council. He is called The Theologian because of his writings on the Trinity and his spiritual poetry. Many of his sermons and letters still exist and are a valuable record of theological thought in the early Church. He died about 389.

A Father of the Church, St. Gregory was called the Wonder Worker because of the many miracles he wrought in his lifetime. His miracles are said to have converted the city of Neocaesarea in Asia Minor where he was bishop. He was also a man of great virtue. He died about 272.

Other saints with this name:

St. Gregory of Tours (France) *Nov. 17*
St. Gregory Grassi (China) *July 7*
Bl. Gregory Lopez (Mexico) *July 20*


# Guy *(Old French:* Guide)                    Sept. 12

### Another Form: Guido

St. Guy was a poor youth who lived near Brussels, Belgium. For some years he was sacristan in the church at Lacken. He decided to make a pilgrimage to Jerusalem, no easy feat in those days. On the way back he passed through Rome, where he met the Vicar of Anderlecht, who was leading a group of pilgrims to the Holy Land. Guy offered to serve as their guide. The group reached Jerusalem safely, but on the way back home plague struck the travelers, and all died except Guy. Sick and exhausted from the two journeys, Guy finally reached Anderlecht to tell of what had happened. There he died in 1012. He is invoked for the protection of dogs and against rabies. He is the patron of those with epilepsy.

Another saint with this name:

Bl. Guy of Cortona (Italy) *June 12*


# Harold *(Danish:* Strong Warrior)                    Nov. 1

St. Harold was the first Christian King of Denmark. He sought to convert his people to Christianity and was put to death by pagan idolaters who had revolted because of his religion. He died in 980 A.D.


# Harvey *(Teutonic:* Warrior)                    June 17

### Another Form: Hervé

St. Harvey, or Hervé, as he is called in France, is a popular saint in Brittany. He was born blind, and his mother entrusted his education to an uncle who had a small monastic school. St. Harvey decided to become a monk and eventually was put in charge of his uncle's monastery. As the monastery grew, St. Harvey led a group of monks and scholars to found a new monastery. He became well known for his preaching and even in his lifetime was called a saint by the people. He died about 550.

# Henry (*Teutonic:* Home Ruler) July 15

**Other Forms: Emeric, Enrico, Harry, Heinrich, Henri, Rico**

St. Henry the Emperor was born in Bavaria, Germany, in 973. He succeeded his father as Duke of Bavaria, and because of his outstanding qualities he was elected emperor of the Holy Roman Empire, which included most of Germany, Austria, Switzerland, Belgium, Holland, and the north of Italy. He was consecrated emperor at Mainz, June 16, 1007. He is called "the most Christian prince" because of his work for the Church. Henry brought about necessary reforms, protected the papacy, encouraged missionary activity, founded monasteries and dioceses. In his own life he gave great Christian example, practicing the Gospel virtues.

Other saints with this name:

St. Henry the Hermit (Denmark) *July 16*
Bl. Henry Suso (Germany) *Mar. 2*

# Herbert (*Teutonic:* Shining Warrior) Mar. 20

St. Herbert was an English hermit who was a close friend of the great monk St. Cuthbert. He lived on an island in Lake Derwentwater where he practiced all sorts of penances and fasting. He often prayed that he would die on the same day as his friend Cuthbert. This grace was granted him when both men died on the same day in 687.

# Herman (*Teutonic:* Soldier) Apr. 7

**Other Forms: Armand, Armando, Ernan, Germain, German, Hermann, Herme, Hernando**

Bl. Herman Joseph is known not only for his own holy life but for his ability to read the hearts of people who came to him for spiritual advice. He was born in Cologne, Germany, and as a youth entered the Premonstratensian Order to study for the priesthood. He was a man of much prayer, spending long hours in chapel. He had great devotion to the Blessed Virgin and is reputed to have had visions and conversations with her. Despite the harshness he imposed upon himself, he lived to be almost a hundred. He died in 1241.

# Hilarion (*Latin:* Merry)

## Other Forms: Hilaire, Hilary

### ST. HILARION (Oct. 21)

Born of pagan parents in Egypt, Hilarion was converted and baptized when he was 15 years old. During a journey into the desert, he came upon St. Anthony, the Hermit of the Desert. He was so impressed by the life of this holy man, that when he returned to Alexandria, he gave his possessions to the poor and went to live on a marshy island. His holy life attracted other monks who came to him for advice, as well as many pilgrims. So many people were coming to him that he decided to move away to find solitude. He went to Greece, Dalmatia, and Sicily, each time being forced to move on because of the crowds that followed him. He finally settled on a remote mountain peak in Cyprus where he worshipped God until he died about 372.

### ST. HILARY OF POITIERS (Jan. 13)

St. Hilary is a Doctor (Teacher) of the Church. He was born of a rich pagan family and was not converted to Christianity until he was 35 years old. He was elected Bishop of Poitiers and spent the rest of his life opposing the Arian heresy which denied the truth of the Trinity. Because of his zeal, he was exiled for four years by the Emperor Constantine. He is credited with ridding Gaul of Arianism. He wrote many works on Scripture and the Catholic Faith. He died in 367. He is invoked for protection against snakes.

# Hubert (*Teutonic:* Bright Mind) Nov. 3

## Another Form: Umberto

St. Hubert is a popular saint of the Middle Ages who is invoked against rabies and for the protection of dogs. He is patron of hunters, foresters, furriers and makers of precision instruments. He became Bishop of Tongres in Belgium in 705 and was a very popular bishop. He traveled widely through his big diocese, sometimes on horseback and sometimes

*ST. JEROME*

by boat. He replaced shrines to idols with Christian sanctuaries. He was particularly devoted to prisoners and is said to have smuggled food to them through the windows of their cells. He died near Brussels in 727.

# Hugh (*Teutonic:* Thought) Apr. 1

### Other Forms: Hughes, Hugo, Ugo

St. Hugh is a man who wanted to be a monk but instead had to be a bishop. He was appointed to the post of Bishop of Grenoble in 1080. He once withdrew to a monastery, but the Pope told him to go back to his job. About six years after he became bishop, Saint Bruno and six companions came to Grenoble looking for a hermitage. Hugh led them to the wildest and remotest place in his diocese, and there the famous abbey of Grand Chartreuse was founded, to which Hugh came as often as he could to share the life of the monks. Hugh never used a horse, traveling his diocese by foot. He sold his possessions to give money to the poor. He was a popular preacher. He died in 1131.

# Ignatius (*Greek:* Fiery)

### Other Forms: Ignace, Ignacio, Ignazio, Iñigo, Nacho

ST. IGNATIUS OF ANTIOCH (Oct. 17)

St. Ignatius was the second Bishop of Antioch, succeeding St. Peter. In the persecution of Trajan he was arrested and taken to Rome to be put to death, enduring many trials on the way. During the journey he wrote seven letters to the various churches which are valuable records of his time and show the development of theology in the early Church. In Rome he was taken to the Colosseum, where he was thrown to wild beasts. Two lions devoured him.

ST. IGNATIUS LOYOLA (July 31)

St. Ignatius was born in Loyola, Spain, in 1491. He joined the army and became a captain of artillery. In the siege of Pamplona, he was gravely wounded when a cannonball struck his leg. Taken to the Castle of Loyola for his recovery, he could find only two books to help him pass the time. One was a life of Christ and the other the lives of saints. After reading these books, he resolved he would serve Christ and His Mother as faithfully as he had served the queen. He went to the University of Paris to study to become a priest. There he gathered a small group of young men about him whom he formed into the Society of Jesus (the Jesuits). The Society grew with speed and importance. He died in Rome in 1556.

# Isaac (*Hebrew:* He Laughs)      Oct. 19

St. Isaac Jogues was born in Orleans, France. He became a Jesuit and after ordination was sent to Canada to do mission work. He was captured in New York State by the Mohawk Indians of the Iroquois Tribe. He was taken captive to Auriesville, N.Y., where he was tortured. During the torture several fingers were chewed off by women. St. Isaac later escaped and made his way down the Hudson River to New York where he returned to France to regain his health. He came back to America. While seeking a way to preach to the Mohawks, he was again captured in New York State and this time was put to death.


# Isidore (*Greek:* Strong Gift)      May 10

**Other Forms: Dore, Dorian**

St. Isidore the Farmer is the patron saint of Madrid, Spain. Born into a poor family, he spent his life as a workman and became a saint through his love of God and the sanctification of daily tasks. He died in 1170, and his body was later found to be incorrupt. Because the ordinary Spanish people could identify with him, Isidore became a very popular saint among them. Spanish colonists brought devotion to him to the New World, and he became popular among the Indians.

Other saints with this name:

St. Isidore of Seville (Spain) *Apr. 4*
St. Isidore of Egypt, *Jan. 15*
St. Isidore, Martyr (Egypt) *May 15*


# Ives (*Teutonic:* Archer)      May 19

**Other Forms: Ivar, Iver, Ivo, Ivor, Yves**

St. Ives was born in the Breton region of France and became a man of many careers. He was a priest, pastor, lawyer, and judge. He had a great love of St. Francis of Assisi and tried to imitate him in his life. He wore coarse clothing, gave alms to the poor and unfortunate, supported orphans by taking them into his own home. He died in 1303.

# James (English form of Jacob [*Hebrew:* Supplanter])

**Other Forms: Diego, Iago, Jacob, Jacques, Jaime, Santiago, Seàmas, Shamus, Yakov**

## ST. JAMES, BROTHER OF ST. JOHN (July 25)

St. James the Apostle, brother of St. John, is sometimes called James the Greater to distinguish him from another Apostle by the same name (James the Less). He was a fisherman and a son of Zebedee. He and his brother John were mending nets with their father when Jesus called upon them to follow Him. Because of the fiery nature of these two brothers, Jesus called them "Sons of Thunder." James along with John and Peter was allowed to see the Transfiguration of Jesus. One day his mother went to Jesus to ask that her sons receive special honor in Jesus' kingdom. He told her that they would have to suffer with Him but that they would have to earn any honors. According to legend, St. James went to Spain after the death of Jesus and preached the Gospel. Called back to Jerusalem, he returned with some disciples. There he was arrested by Herod Agrippa and beheaded. His disciples brought his bones back to Spain, burying them in Galicia, where a great shrine was built to him at Compostela which has attracted millions of pilgrims over the centuries. He is the patron of Spain, and the Moslems were driven out under the banner of Santiago (San Iago, or St. James). Many places have been named in his honor, such as Santiago, Chile. He was the first Apostle martyred.

## ST. JAMES, RELATIVE OF THE LORD (May 3)

St. James, sometimes called the Less, was a relative of Jesus, son of Alphaeus, and a cousin of St. Jude. He is called the Less because he was called by Jesus after the other James, not because he was any less important. He wrote an epistle which can be found in the New Testament. He became the first Bishop of Jerusalem and presided over the Church there while the other Apostles went forth preaching the Gospel. He is said to have led a prayerful life of penance. In the year 62 he was arrested by Jewish officials. He was thrown from the Temple roof. Badly injured but not quite dead, he was then stoned.

# Jeremias (*Hebrew:* Exalted of the Lord) May 1

**Other Forms: Geremia, Jeremy, Jeremiah**

Jeremias was one of the major prophets of the Old Testament.

## ST. JEREMY (Feb. 16)

St. Jeremy was a martyr killed in Palestine in the fourth century.

*ST. JOHN THE BAPTIST*

63

# Jerome *(Greek:* Holy Name) Sept. 30

### Other Forms: Geronimo, Hieronymus

St. Jerome is a Doctor (Teacher) of the Church. He was born in Dalmatia and went to Rome to study. There he was baptized. For a time he lived the life of a monk. After he was ordained as priest, he gave himself up to scholarship and study of Scripture. Later Jerome returned to Rome and became secretary for Pope Damasus, who ordered him to prepare a Latin translation of the Bible. Jerome went to Bethlehem and for the next thirty years worked to produce the Latin Vulgate translation which has been in use to our own times. He also wrote on many theological and scriptural subjects. Jerome died in Bethlehem in 420. He is a patron of students.

Another saint by this name:

St. Jerome Emiliani (Italy) *Feb. 8*


# Joachim *(Hebrew:* God Prepares) July 26

### Another Form: Joaquin

Joachim is the name given to the father of the Blessed Virgin Mary. Devotion to the parents of Mary is an ancient one in the Eastern Churches and more recently in the West.


# Joel *(Hebrew:* The Coming Down of God) July 13

St. Joel was one of the twelve minor prophets of the Old Testament, and his prophecy may be read there. He foretells of the evils that were to fall upon the Jews but promises that God will send them a teacher of justice (Jesus Christ) and the Holy Spirit. He prophesied around the year 780 B.C.


# John *(Hebrew:* God Has Mercy)

### Other Forms: Baptiste, Evan, Gian, Giovanni, Hans, Ian, Ivan, Jan, Johann, Johannes, Jon, Juan, Seàn, Shane, Shaun

## ST. JOHN THE BAPTIST                    (June 24, Aug. 29)

John the Baptist was the son of Zachary, a temple priest, and Elizabeth, a cousin of Jesus Christ. His birth was surrounded by miraculous happenings (see Gospel of Luke, chapter 1). His purpose in life was to prepare the way for Jesus by preaching penance. As a young man, he retired to the desert to live there on locusts and wild honey. When Jesus came to John to be baptized, John called Jesus "the Lamb of God." Some of John's disciples left him to follow Jesus. Not long after, he was arrested by Herod and then beheaded through the trickery of Salome (see the Gospel of St. Mark, chapter 6). Jesus said of him: "Among those born of women, none is greater than John."

## ST. JOHN THE APOSTLE AND EVANGELIST              (Dec. 27)

St. John, Apostle and Evangelist, was a disciple of St. John the Baptist when he first met Jesus. Later while he was repairing nets at the Sea of Galilee with his brother James, the two of them were invited by the Master to follow Him as His disciples. He became very beloved to Jesus, was with Him at the Transfiguration, and next to Him at the Last Supper. On the Cross, Jesus gave His mother, Mary, to the safekeeping of John. After the death of Jesus, John and Peter worked together closely. Later John was arrested and exiled. It was reported that he was plunged into boiling oil but miraculously saved. He went to Asia Minor to live and teach, wrote his Gospel and Epistles and the Book of Revelations. He died as a very old man, still teaching the love of Jesus.

There are more saints with the name of John than with any other name. Some of them are:

St. John Baptist de la Salle (France) *Apr. 7*
St. John Bosco (Italy) *Jan. 31*
St. John Capistrano (Italy) *Mar. 28*
St. John Chrysostom (Syria) *Sept. 13*
St. John de Brebeuf (United States) *Oct. 19*
St. John Fisher (England) *June 22*
St. John Neumann (United States) *Jan. 5*
St. John of the Cross (Spain) *Dec. 14*
St. John of God (Portugal) *Mar. 8*
St. John Vianney (France) *Aug. 4*

# Joseph *(Hebrew:* Increase)                    Mar. 19

### Other Forms: Giuseppe, José, Josef

St. Joseph was the husband of the Blessed Virgin Mary and foster father of Our Lord Jesus Christ. He was a carpenter in the town of Nazareth. He was a descendant of the line of King David, and the New Testa-

*ST. JOSEPH*

ment calls him "a just man." He was advised in a dream about the child Mary was to have, and he took her with him when he went to Bethlehem to enroll in a census that was being taken. There Jesus was born in a stable because all the inns were crowded. Joseph was warned in a dream to flee with Mary and the child to Egypt to escape the jealousy of Herod. After a period of exile there, he returned with Jesus and Mary to Nazareth. Each year it was his custom to take Jesus and Mary to Jerusalem for the Passover. They made this journey when Jesus was twelve years old, and on the way back to Nazareth they missed the boy, each thinking that He was with the other. They returned to Jerusalem and after three days found Jesus teaching in the Temple. They returned to Nazareth, and sometime after this Joseph died. The Church holds St. Joseph in great honor because of his care for Jesus and his love for Mary. He is patron of carpenters and is prayed to for a good death.

Other saints with this name:

St. Joseph Calasanz (Spain) *Aug. 25*
St. Joseph Benedict Cottolengo (Italy) *Apr. 30*
St. Joseph Cupertino (Italy) *Sept. 18*


# Jude (*Hebrew:* Praised)      Oct. 28

St. Jude is one of the Twelve Apostles. He is the son of James, not otherwise identified. St. Mark gives him also the name of Thaddeus. At the Last Supper he was the one who asked Jesus why He had revealed Himself only to the disciples and not to the whole world. According to tradition he preached the Gospel in Persia with St. Simon and was martyred there. He is invoked for desperate cases.


# Julius (*Latin:* Soft Beard)      Apr. 12

## Other Forms: Giles, Giulio, Jules, Julian, Julio

Pope St. Julius I was a Roman citizen who was elected in 337. His papacy was filled with many trials because of heretics. He was a defender of St. Athanasius, who had been driven from his see in Alexandria because of his fight against the Arian heretics. Pope Julian died in 352 and was buried in the catacomb of St. Callixtus.

Another saint with this name:

St. Julian of Toledo (Spain) *Mar. 8*

# Justin *(Latin:* Just)                                         Aug. 1

Justin was a young Christian boy in France who died as a martyr. One day he and his father were making a trip from Paris to Amiens when a band of men searching for Christians came on them. Justin's father escaped and hid, but Justin was caught. Despite being beaten, he refused to tell the men in what direction his father had gone, and he likewise refused to deny that he was a Christian. The men killed the boy when they could get nothing from him. He died about 288 A.D.


# Kenneth *(Celtic:* Handsome)                                  Oct. 11

### Other Forms: Canice, Kent

St. Kenneth is the patron of Kilkenny, Ireland. He was a friend and follower of St. Columba. He later left the monastery of Iona and settled in the diocese of Ossory, where he founded the church at Kilkenny. He died in the year 600.


# Kevin *(Gaelic:* Handsome)                                    June 3

St. Kevin is one of the patrons of Dublin, Ireland. He is said to have been of royal descent. He was educated by Irish monks, became a priest, and decided to be a hermit. His holiness and cures of the sick brought him many disciples, so he founded the Abbey of Glendalough, which became a place of pilgrimage. He lived to an old age, dying in 618.


# Kieran *(Gaelic:* Black)                                      Mar. 5

St. Kieran was a contemporary of St. Patrick and is called by the Irish their first native-born saint. Both Ossory and Cork claim to be his birthplace. He received an elementary education in Christianity and then went to Rome to be more fully instructed. According to ancient accounts, it was on this trip that he first met St. Patrick. When Patrick came to Ireland, St. Kieran was one of the twelve men he appointed bishops to assist him. St. Kieran is venerated as the first Bishop of Ossory and died about 530.

*ST. LAWRENCE*

# Killian (*Celtic:* Church) July 8

**Another Form: Kilian**

St. Killian was an Irish missioner who went to preach the Gospel in Thuringia, Germany, along with St. Colman. They were both put to death there for their efforts about 689.

# Ladislas (*Slavic:* Ruling Well) June 27

**Other Forms: Ladislaus, Lance, Lancelot, Lazlo, Vladislas**

St. Ladislas is a great figure in Hungarian history. He succeeded to the throne in 1077 and had to put down rebellions, drive the Tartars back to Russia, and fight the Serbs and Bulgars. He acted always in the best interests of his people. A huge man, he was very popular with the soldiers he led into battle. He was a man of great wisdom, and when it came time for the West to choose a leader for the First Crusade, the French, English, and Spanish unanimously selected Ladislas. He accepted but died in 1095 before he could take the expedition to the Holy Land. He was a man of great virtue who tried always to do the will of God.

# Lawrence (*Latin:* Laurel) Aug. 10

**Other Forms: Lars, Lauren, Laurence, Laurenz, Lauritz, Loren, Lorenzo**

St. Lawrence was a deacon who was martyred, and devotion to him became widespread in Europe. Lawrence was an assistant to Pope Sixtus II. In 258 the Emperor Valerian issued an edict against Christians which declared that all Christians would be put to death and their property confiscated. One of the first arrested was Pope Sixtus. Lawrence then was brought before the Prefect of Rome and ordered to deliver up all the wealth of the Church. He asked for a delay and used the time to give alms to the poor. The next day he returned to the prefect, followed by beggars. "Here is the wealth of the Church," Lawrence told the prefect. Angered at having been tricked, the prefect ordered that Lawrence should be roasted to death over a slow fire. St. Ambrose tells us that even in death Lawrence kept his humor. "I'm well done on this side," he told his tormentors. "Turn me over to the other." He died praying for the city of Rome. He is patron of cooks and invoked against fire.

Other saints with this name:

St. Lawrence of Brindisi (Italy) *July 21*
St. Lawrence Justinian (Italy) *Sept. 5*
St. Laurence O'Toole (Ireland) *Nov. 14*

# Leo (*Latin:* Lion) Nov. 10

### Other Forms: Lee, Lon, Leov, Lionel

Pope St. Leo the Great ruled the Church in one of its greatest periods of upheaval. A native of Rome, he became pope in 440. The Church at the time was afflicted by many heresies — Pelagianism, Nestorianism, Manichaeanism, and others. At the same time the Roman Empire was being attacked by Huns, Goths, Visigoths and Vandals. On one occasion, St. Leo rode out to meet Atilla the Hun and persuaded him not to advance on Rome. During this confusing period, St. Leo held the Church together, strengthened the authority of the papacy and at the same time lived a life of holiness. He died in 461.

# Leonard (*Teutonic:* Lionhearted) Nov. 6

### Other Forms: Leon, Leonardo, Leonhard

St. Leonard is the patron of prisoners. He was a Frankish lord who fought alongside the king, Clovis. With Clovis he was baptized at Rheims in 496. Clovis wished to make him a bishop, but Leonard refused. He did not wish even to be a priest, although he allowed himself to be ordained a deacon. He asked Clovis for permission to visit the prisons and to free those he found deserving. Clovis granted his wish, and he spent most of the remainder of his life working among captives and prisoners. He built a sanctuary in a forest and there gathered disciples around him, many of them former prisoners. He died about 599.

# Leopold (*German:* People's Prince) Nov. 15

### Another Form: Leopoldo

To St. Leopold's name is usually added the phrase, "The Pious," because of his holy life. He was born into the Austrian nobility. He was the grandson of Emperor Henry III; one of his sons became Emperor Conrad, and another was the father of the famous Frederick Barbarossa. He was a brave general of the Austrian army who drove back Hungarian invaders. He died in 1136, respected and loved by the people.

# Louis (*Teutonic:* Famous Warrior)                    Aug. 25

**Other Forms: Alois, Aloysius (see), Lewis, Ludovico, Ludwig, Luigi, Luis**

St. Louis, King of France, was the leader of the seventh and eighth Crusades. He became king when only eleven years old and took the name of Louis IX. He had six sons and five daughters. Falling sick, Louis vowed he would lead a crusade to the Holy Land if he recovered. He did and organized an army which he landed in Egypt in 1246. After some early successes, he was captured by the Moslems. He gave back one of the places he had captured as ransom and was allowed to go on to Jerusalem. He returned to France in 1254 and set about developing his kingdom, building hospitals, Sainte Chapelle, and starting the Sorbonne University. He had the respect of all the kings of Europe and was considered a saint by the people. St. Louis became a blacksmith to identify with the working people. He died in 1270 while preparing to attack Tunis on his last crusade. His remains were brought back to Paris and buried in the Church of St. Denis. He is patron of builders and other workers.


# Luke (*Greek:* Light)                                (Oct. 18)

**Other Forms: Luc, Luca, Lucas, Lucian, Luciano, Lucio, Lucius**

St. Luke was the only evangelist who was not a Jew. He belonged to the Greek world, and St. Paul refers to him as "beloved Luke, the physician." He was converted by St. Paul when Paul and Barnabas came to Antioch to preach Christianity. He became a scribe and companion to St. Paul and remained with the Apostle of the Gentiles throughout his captivity. Saint Luke wrote the third Gospel, based on what St. Paul and others told him. He did make one journey to Jerusalem with Paul, and it is thought that while there he interviewed the Blessed Mother. His Gospel has much material not found in the other Gospels, particularly about the infancy of Christ. He also wrote The Acts of the Apostles which tells of life in the early Church and of the work of Peter and Paul. There is no record of when he died, but some historians believe he died naturally in Rome. He is patron of doctors and artists.


# Malachy (*Hebrew:* Messenger of the Lord)            Nov. 2

**Another Form: Malachi**

St. Malachy was born in Armagh, Ireland. He became a priest and then abbot at Connor. He was appointed Archbishop of Armagh, but he gave way to a rival. A very holy man who suffered many trials and who is said to have worked miracles in his lifetime, he was respected by the people. On a trip to Rome, he visited the Abbey of Clairvaux in France and there died in 1148 in the presence of his friend, St. Bernard.


# Mark *(Latin:* Of Mars) Apr. 25

## Other Forms: Marc, Marcel, Marco, Marcus, Markus

St. Mark, sometimes referred to in the New Testament as John Mark, was a cousin of St. Barnabas and a native of Jerusalem. His mother, Mary, was a Christian, and her house was a meeting place for early Christians. Some think that it was in her house that the Last Supper was held. Some Scripture scholars identify Mark with the young man in his Gospel who ran away naked when Christ was arrested in the Garden. Others believe he was baptized by St. Peter, who calls him "his son." In the year 44, Mark joined Sts. Paul and Barnabas on a missionary journey going to Cyprus and Asia Minor. Later he was to make another trip with Barnabas and still later was with Paul in Rome. It is believed that he gathered most of the material for his Gospel, which was the first one written, perhaps as early as 50 A.D., from St. Peter. Egyptian Copts claim St. Mark as the founder of the Church in Egypt. Tradition also says he died during the persecution of Trajan. He is patron of lawyers and invoked against the loss of faith.


# Martin *(Latin:* Warlike)

## Another Form: Martino

ST. MARTIN DE PORRES (Nov. 3)

St. Martin was born in Lima, Peru, to a Spanish father and Black mother. As a boy he learned the basics of medicine in an apprenticeship and then he entered the Dominican monastery as a lay brother. He worked for the city's poor, begging for their needs and using his medical skills in their illnesses. He was given to fervent prayer and once prayed through an earthquake without noticing it. He had a particular devotion to the Holy Eucharist. Like St. Francis, he had a special way with animals, and he used to gather the mice each day to feed them. He is reputed to have worked many miracles in his life. He died in 1639. He has been named patron of Black people.

73

## ST. MARTIN OF TOURS (Nov. 11)

St. Martin of Tours was a soldier. When he was about twenty, he was baptized and left the army to serve St. Hilary of Poitiers. Later he retired to become a monk and helped found Ligugé, the most ancient monastery in the West. When in 371 the people of Tours were seeking a bishop, they elected Martin by acclamation. He was soon noted for his praying, preaching, and good works. He traveled widely through France, converting whole districts. Whenever he converted an area, he would leave behind monks and priests to build up the Church. When he died in 397, Martin was so popular that hundreds of villages were named after him and it is said that 4,000 churches were dedicated to him in France alone. He is the patron of horsemen.

# Matthew (*Hebrew:* The Lord's Gift)

### Other Forms: Matt, Matteo, Matthäus, Matthias

## ST. MATTHEW (Sept. 21)

St. Matthew, Apostle and Evangelist, was a tax collector called Levi, when Jesus invited him to become an Apostle. He was a native of Capernaum where Jesus did His early preaching. After the death of Jesus, he wrote his Gospel in Aramaic for the Palestinian Jews to show that Jesus was the promised Messiah. Tradition says that he preached the Gospel in the East and was martyred there.

## ST. MATTHIAS (May 14)

St. Matthias was the Apostle who was chosen to take the place of Judas. He had been a disciple of Jesus and had traveled about Palestine with the Master. After Jesus had ascended to heaven, the eleven Apostles met in Jerusalem to pick a successor to the traitor Judas. Two men were nominated, Justus and Matthias. A vote was taken and Matthias was elected. There are two traditions about St. Matthias. One is that he preached the Gospel in Ethiopia and was put to death there, another that he was martyred in Palestine. He is the patron of tailors and alcoholics.

# Maurice (*Greek:* Dark) Sept. 22

### Other Forms: Maur, Mauricio, Maurizio, Moritz, Morris

Maurice was an Egyptian, a member of Rome's Theban Legion. In 286 there was an uprising against Rome in Gaul. The Theban Legion, along with other troops, was sent from Italy over the Alps to put down the

*ST. MARTIN OF TOURS*

disturbance. Before going into battle, the commander ordered his troops to sacrifice to the gods. Maurice and some other Christian soldiers refused, and they were put to death.

# Maximilian (*Latin:* Greatest) Oct. 12

**Other Forms: Max, Massimiliano, Maxim**

St. Maximilian was a native of the Austro-German area of Europe. After working as a lay missioner, he became a priest and was later appointed Bishop of Lorsch. While visiting his territory he was arrested for being a Christian. He was ordered to offer sacrifice to the god Mars. When he refused, he was put to death (about 281).

# Meinrad (*Teutonic:* Strong Firmness) Jan. 21

**Another Form: Maynard**

St. Meinrad was born into a noble family in what is now Germany about 800. He became a monk and a priest at the Abbey of Reichenau, where he taught Sacred Scripture. Feeling that monastic life was not strict enough for him, he received permission to live as a hermit. For seven years he lived on a mountain peak overlooking Lake Zurich. Then he left to make a hermitage in a remote forest, taking with him a statue of the Virgin. The spot is now a place of pilgrimage to Our Lady of Einsiedlen, Meinrad's statue. St. Meinrad was killed in 861 by bandits.

# Mel (Gaelic, from *Latin:* Honey) Feb. 6

St. Mel is one of the earliest Irish saints. He was a nephew of St. Patrick, whom he assisted in his work. He became a priest and was appointed the first Bishop of Armagh. He built a great monastery there which he also served as abbot. He was the one who received the great St. Brigit into the religious life. He died about 490.

*ST. MARTIN DE PORRES*

*ST. MATTHEW*

# Michael (*Hebrew:* Who is Like God?)     Sept. 29

**Other Forms: Michel, Michele, Miguel, Mikhail, Mitchell**

St. Michael the Archangel is one of the three angels mentioned by name in the Bible. The Prophet Daniel describes him as the heavenly prince who stands guard over God's people. He is considered the leader of God's powers against Satan. Michael has always been popular with Christians of both East and West. Many churches have been built in his honor, one of the most famous being Mont Saint Michel, which was erected in 709 in Normandy, France. He is patron of policemen.

# Moses (*Hebrew:* Saved from Water)     Aug. 28

St. Moses is one of the earliest recorded Black saints. Born in Abyssinia as a slave, he had a vile temper and nasty disposition. He became so troublesome and mean that as a young man he was driven from his master's estate. He then became a robber and headed up a band of highwaymen that preyed upon travelers going to and from Egypt. Somehow (the details are lost) he was converted to Christianity, and his life then became one of penance. He joined a monastery in Lower Egypt, became a priest, and was one of the foremost Fathers of the Desert. He had many disciples when he died near the end of the fifth century.

# Nathaniel (*Hebrew:* Gift of God)     Aug. 24

**Another Form: Nathanael**

Nathaniel is believed to be another name for St. Bartholomew the Apostle (*see*). It was not uncommon for a Jew to have two names and to be known by either or both of them. He is introduced under this name when the Apostle Philip brings him to Jesus who confounds him with what He already knows. Jesus promises Nathaniel that he will see great things. You can read the incident in the first chapter of the Gospel of John.

# Nicholas (*Greek:* People's Victory)     Dec. 6

**Other Forms: Claus, Colin, Klaus, Nicol, Nicolò, Nikolaus, Niles, Nils**

St. Nicholas is one of the most popular saints of the early Church, and many early writers speak of his greatness. There are many stories of miracles he worked in his lifetime. After some years as a monk, he became Archbishop of Myra, Turkey. One story told about him relates to the time he was on his way to the Council of Nicaea. He stopped at an inn to spend the night where the owner had killed two boys to steal from them the little money they carried. Nicholas discovered the crime, brought the boys back to life and had the innkeeper arrested. For this and other acts he is considered the patron of children. He is the one who supposedly brought presents to children at Christmas, whom children today call Santa Claus (Saint Claus, or Nicholas). He died about 324.

Other saints with this name:

St. Nicholas of Tolentine (Italy) *Sept. 10*
St. Nicholas of Umbria (Italy) *Oct. 10*


# Noel *(French:* Christmas) Feb. 21

Blessed Noel Pinot was a martyr in the French revolution. One of sixteen children, he became a priest in 1771. For a time he served as a chaplain of a hospital and then became a pastor, using the income from his parish to aid the poor. When the revolutionary tribunal told him to take the oath to the revolutionary government which was opposed to the Church, Noel refused. Driven from his parish, he was forced to go into hiding. He did not desert his people but hid by day and said Mass and heard confession by night. One night as he was saying Mass at a farm, he was discovered and arrested. He was sentenced to death and on the same day, Feb. 21, 1794, had his head chopped off by the guillotine.


# Norbert *(French:* Brightness) June 6

St. Norbert was a handsome young man of noble German birth who allowed himself to become a subdeacon in order to gain ecclesiastical honors. He led a worldly life until he was 33 years old. Then while riding one day he was struck by lightning. Because of this close brush with death, he gave away his possessions, became a priest, dressed in poor clothes, and went about preaching against the life he had once led. Accused by enemies of slandering the clergy, Norbert was brought before Pope Gelasius, who heard his story and authorized him to preach anywhere in the Catholic Church. With some friends he founded the Premonstratensian Order to restore religious life among clergy and people. He was later made a bishop, and he died in 1134.

*ST. MICHAEL THE ARCHANGEL*

81

# Oliver *(Latin:* Peace)                              July 10

St. Oliver Plunkett was born in Ireland during the time James I and Oliver Cromwell of England were trying to make the country Protestant. Because of the lack of educational opportunities for Irish boys, he was sent to the Irish College in Rome when he was 16. There he became a priest and worked in the Holy City until Pope Clement IX named him Archbishop of Armagh. In Ireland he worked under great difficulty because of persecution by the English. Finally he was accused by renegades of conspiracy against the British. He was taken to England and put on trial. The witnesses against him perjured themselves and told fantastic lies. It was enough for the British to condemn him to death. He greeted his sentence of hanging by saying, "It is good for me at this time to give an example to the Irish people since I have already given them so much advice." He was executed at the infamous Tyburn Prison in 1681.

# Otto *(Teutonic:* Rich)                              July 2

**Other Forms: Odo, Odilo**

St. Otto was a priest who became chancellor of the German Empire. He was a friend of kings and popes. When King Boleslaus conquered Pomerania, he called for missioners to preach the Gospel there. Otto and some companions answered the call and went to Pomerania (Poland). In one year Otto baptized 20,000 people and built eleven churches. He died in 1139.

# Owen *(Middle English:* To Possess)                   Mar. 3

St. Owen was an Anglo-Saxon monk who with St. Chad worked to serve the people of England, particularly the poor. He labored in the area of Lichfield. St. Owen led a very holy life and is reputed to have had visions of Jesus and heaven. He died about 680, and the people among whom he worked proclaimed him a saint.

# Pascal (*Hebrew:* Passover)                                    May 17

### Other Forms: Paschal, Pasquale

St. Pascal Baylon was born in Aragon (Spain) in 1540 of parents who were farmers. From the time he was a boy until he became a young man, he was a shepherd. When he was about 27 years old, he became a Franciscan Brother, serving as cook, gardener, and porter. He served the poor in many ways but particularly by his healing powers. He worked many miracles in his lifetime, and during the process of canonization St. Robert Bellarmine told the court, "His like has not been seen in the world." Because of his devotion to the Holy Eucharist, Pope Leo XIII named him special patron of Eucharistic congresses.


# Patrick (*Latin:* Nobly Born)                                   Mar. 17

### Other Forms: Padraic, Patrice, Patricio, Patriztus

St. Patrick was born in Great Britain about 385. When he was about sixteen, he was captured by pirates and taken to Ireland as a slave, working as a shepherd. Patrick escaped and returned home. The paganism of Ireland disturbed Patrick, and he resolved to become a priest and to return there to preach the Gospel. When he did go back, it was as a bishop. Patrick went to Tara which was the seat of the Irish kings and the pagan Druid priests. It was at the time of the vernal equinox when all the fires in Ireland were supposed to be extinguished until the Druids made new fire. On a hill overlooking Tara, Patrick built a huge bonfire to announce the Resurrection. The next day he went to Tara, debated the Druids whom he overcame. Then plucking a shamrock from the ground, he used its three leaves to explain the Trinity to the kings. Patrick was tireless in preaching the Gospel, and he converted many, many thousands to the Faith. St. Patrick organized the Church through Ireland, lived a life of penance and wrote many prayers (some of which still remain for us). He died in 461.


# Paul (*Latin:* Little)                                          June 29

### Other Forms: Pablo, Paolo, Paulinus, Paulo, Pawel

Paul was born in Tarsus, Cilicia, a fact which gave him Roman citizenship. His parents, devout Jews, sent him to Jerusalem to study his religion under the noted Rabbi Gamaliel. There he became a Pharisee.

Because of his deep Jewish religious beliefs, he opposed Christianity. He was present approvingly at the stoning to death of Stephen the Deacon, the first martyr. He was on his way to Damascus to arrest Christians when he was struck to the ground and Christ appeared to him. From that moment on he devoted himself entirely to the spread of Christianity. Along with Peter he became the leading figure in the early Church and no one did as much as he to shape Christianity. His missionary journeys took him through Asia Minor, Greece, Mediterranean islands and finally to Rome as a prisoner. Attempts were made on his life; he was imprisoned and beaten. He was freed from his first Roman imprisonment. Then he was rearrested by agents of Nero, taken again to Rome, where because he was a Roman citizen he was beheaded, not crucified, about three years after St. Peter. His many epistles give the basis for Catholic teaching. According to Eusebius, he was martyred in the year 67.

Other saints with this name:

St. Paul Miki (Japan) *Feb. 6*
St. Paul of Damascus (Syria) *Sept. 25*
St. Paulinus of Nola (Italy) *June 22*
St. Paul of Rome (Italy) *June 26*

# Peter (*Greek:* Rock)           June 29

### Other Forms: Pedro, Perrin, Petrus, Pierce, Pierre, Piers, Pietro, Piotr

It was at the Jordan River that St. Peter first met Jesus. He was there with his brother Andrew, who first told him about Jesus. Peter and Andrew were fishermen from Bethsaida, a town on the north shore of the Sea of Galilee. When Jesus began His public life, He called Simon and Andrew to follow Him. Jesus changed his name from Simon to Rock, telling him that he was the rock on which Jesus would found His Church. Peter was present at all the important Gospel incidents and was chosen by Jesus to witness His Transfiguration. Peter began Christ's Passion boldly enough, cutting off the ear of one who would arrest Jesus. Then he became afraid and three times denied that he even knew Christ. Jesus forgave him and after the Resurrection three times ordered Peter to take care of the people in the Church. On Pentecost, Peter was the chief spokesman for the Apostles. The Acts of the Apostles tell of his miracles and leadership. He was arrested about 43 A.D. by Herod but miraculously released. He presided over the Council of Jerusalem in the year 50, when it was decided to admit Gentiles to the Church. He became the first Bishop of Antioch, lived for a time in Corinth, then went to Rome where he was crucified upside down during the persecution of Nero. His tomb is beneath the main altar of St. Peter's Basilica in Rome. He was the first Pope, and the

ST. PATRICK

Church holds that his successors have the same powers as Christ gave Peter, which are necessary for the Church with which Christ promised to remain until the end of time.

St. Peter Baptist (Japan) *Feb. 6*
St. Peter Canisius (Switzerland) *Apr. 27*
St. Peter Claver (Colombia) *Sept. 9*
St. Peter Chanel (Oceania) *Apr. 28*
St. Peter Damian (Italy) *Feb. 21*
St. Peter Julian Eymard (France) *Aug. 3*
St. Peter Nolasco (Spain) *Jan. 31*

# Philip *(Greek:* Lover of Horses)

## Other Forms: Felipe, Filippo, Phelps, Philipp, Philippe, Philippus

### ST. PHILIP THE APOSTLE                                    (May 3)

St. Philip, a native of Bethsaida, was in Galilee when Jesus called upon him to become His follower. It was Philip who told Nathaniel that he had found the one of whom Moses had written. Nathaniel replied, "Can anything good come from Nazareth?" Philip brought Nathaniel to Jesus, who won him over and made him the Apostle Bartholomew. Philip was the one who helped Jesus at the miracle of feeding the five thousand. Jesus tested Philip by asking him how they were to feed the large crowd. Philip told Jesus that there was a boy in the crowd with a few loaves and fishes, adding, "What is that among so many?" Jesus sent Philip for the boy and with these few loaves and fishes fed the large crowd. At the Last Supper, Philip asked Jesus to show the Apostles the Father. Jesus told Philip, "He who sees me, sees the Father." We do not know how or when St. Philip died.

### ST. PHILIP NERI                                           (May 26)

St. Philip Neri, sometimes called the Apostle of Rome, was born in Florence. He was a gifted man who was skilled in law, chemistry, poetry, music, psychology and theology. He went to Rome in 1536, laboring there as a lay missioner, working with youth, preaching, visiting hospitals, converting rich and poor, a favorite of intellectuals. He helped found the noted Oratory and the Oratorians. He became a priest in 1551. He was so happy in life that he used to cry out, "Enough, Lord! Enough!" He died in 1595.

*ST. PETER*

# Pius *(Latin:* Holy) Aug. 21

### Another Form: Pio

Pius is the name of a number of popes of whom three are saints, the latest being Pope St. Pius X. He was born near Venice in 1835, became a priest, Bishop of Mantua, and then Patriarch of Venice. He was elected pope in 1903. He opposed the errors of Modernism which were sweeping the Church at the time, promoted Gregorian Chant, encouraged frequent Holy Communion and insisted that children be given the sacrament at the age of reason. His whole pontificate was aimed at restoring all things in Christ. He died in 1914.

# Quentin *(Latin:* Fifth) Oct. 31

### Other Forms: Quin, Quinn, Quintus

St. Quentin was the son of a Roman senator. He went with St. Lucian to France to preach the Gospel. He was arrested and imprisoned in Amiens. When he refused to deny Christ, he was tortured and beheaded in a place that afterwards was given his name. He died about 285. In 641, St. Eligius discovered his body, built a handsome tomb for it. St. Quentin is invoked against coughs.

# Ralph *(Teutonic:* Good Omen) July 7

### Other Forms: Rafe, Rafello, Raoul, Raul, Rolfe, Rodolfo, Rudolf, Rudolph (see), Rodolphus

Blessed Ralph Milner was a poor farmer who could not read or write, the father of eight children. He was converted from Protestantism and was arrested on the day of his First Communion. The English judge said that he would free Ralph because of his age and his large number of children if he would go to a nearby Anglican church and say his prayers. Ralph refused, as this would seem that he was denying his new faith. He was executed for his religion at Winchester, England, on July 7, 1591.

# Raphael (*Hebrew:* God's Healer)    Sept. 29

## Other Forms: Rafael, Rafaelle, Raffaello

St. Raphael is one of the three archangels mentioned in the Bible. His story is found in the Book of Tobit. When Tobit decided to send his son, Tobias or Tobiah, to Media to collect a debt, he hired a young man, Raphael, to go along as guide. The journey was made successfully with many adventures, during which the debt was collected, Tobias found a bride and a fortune, and his father had his sight restored. The mysterious young man was the cause of all this good luck. When Tobit wanted to pay him handsomely, the young man declined a reward and revealed: "I am Raphael, one of the seven holy angels who present the prayers of the saints and who enter into the presence of the glory of the holy one." He said that he had come because God had sent him and that he was returning to God. After that Tobit and Tobias saw him no more.

# Raymond (*Teutonic:* Wise Protection)

## Other Forms: Raimondo, Ramon, Raymund, Redmond

### ST. RAYMOND OF PENNAFORT    (Jan. 7)

St. Raymond was a Spaniard who joined the Dominican Order, of which he eventually became head. He was a very learned man in law and wrote a number of works. After a holy and devout life, he died in 1275.

### ST. RAYMOND NONNATUS    (Aug. 31)

St. Raymond was born in Spain and given the baptismal name of Raymond to which was added Nonnatus (not born) because he came into the world through a Caesarian operation and not in the usual manner. He joined the Mercedarian Order, which St. Peter Nolasco had recently founded to rescue captives from the Moslems. He raised ransom money by begging and personally redeemed hundreds of captives in Valencia, Algiers, and Tunisia. In the last place, he ran out of money and gave himself up as a captive in order to free a Christian. After eight months of cruel slave treatment, he himself was rescued by other members of his order. After his release, he urged St. Louis of France to lead a crusade. He was later made a cardinal, dying in 1240. St. Raymond is patron of infants, midwives, and mothers about to give birth.

# Reginald *(Teutonic:* Strong Judgment)      Feb. 17

**Other Forms: Reinhold, Reinwald, Reynold, Rinaldo, Ronald (see)**

Blessed Reginald of Orleans was the first member of the Dominican Order to die. He was born near Arles, France, in 1183. He taught canon law at the University of Paris. While making a pilgrimage to Rome, he met St. Dominic and became his follower. He founded the Dominican priory in Bologna. He was a great preacher and made many recruits for the new Dominican Order. He died in Paris on Feb. 1, 1270.


# René *(French:* Reborn)      Oct. 19

**Other Forms: Renato, Renatus**

St. René Goupil was a Jesuit Oblate who accompanied St. Isaac Jogues when he entered New York State to preach the Gospel. Captured by Mohawk Indians, he and St. Isaac were taken to Auriesville and subjected to cruel torture. He was kept as a slave, but his owner, angered by his prayers, tomahawked him to death in 1642.


# Richard *(Old English:* Firm Ruler)      Apr. 3

**Other Forms: Ricardo, Riccardo**

St. Richard of Chichester was born into a noble but poor family near Worcester, England. After restoring the family fortune and giving his own share to his brother, he went to Europe to study law. Upon his return to England, he was made chancellor of Oxford University and legal advisor to St. Edmund, Archbishop of Canterbury. Later he studied theology and became a priest. He was elected Bishop of Chichester, selling his goods to help the poor and sick. St. Richard was preaching a crusade to recover the burial place of Christ when he fell ill and died in 1253.

Another saint with this name:

St. Richard Gwynn (England) *Oct. 25*

ST. SEBASTIAN

# Robert (*Teutonic:* Bright Flame)                    Sept. 17

## Other Forms: Roberto, Robin, Rupert (see), Ruprecht

St. Robert Bellarmine was a bishop and is honored as Doctor (Teacher) of the Church. He was born in 1542 in Tuscany, Italy. A brilliant student, he entered the Society of Jesus and became a priest. He taught for many years at the Roman College and was recognized as one of the great theologians of the Church and a defender against Protestant teachings. He was made a cardinal and was a papal advisor. He died in 1621.

# Roderic (*Teutonic:* Noble Ruler)                    Mar. 13

## Other Forms: Roderick, Roderico, Rodrigo, Rory, Rurik

St. Roderic was a priest of Cabra, Spain. It was during the time when the Mohammedans controlled much of the country. He was betrayed by his brother who had become a Mohammedan and accused him falsely of deserting the Islamic faith. Roderic told his judge that he was a Christian and had always been a Christian. The judge threw him into prison, telling him that he must deny Christianity. When Roderic continued to refuse to deny his religion, the judge ordered his head to be cut off. He died in 857.

# Roger (*Teutonic:* Famous Spear)                    July 7

## Other Forms: Hodge, Rogelio, Rory, Rudiger, Ruggero

Bl. Roger Dickenson was a native of Lincoln, England, who in order to become a priest had to go to the English College in Rheims, France, because all English seminaries had been closed by the persecution. He had himself smuggled back into England and served the Catholics in the Winchester area. He was caught once but escaped when his guards began drinking. The second time he was arrested along with Blessed Ralph Milner, a lay helper. Both men were executed at Winchester on July 7, 1591.

# Romanus (*Latin:* Roman)  Feb. 28

## Other Forms: Romain, Roman, Romano, Romaric, Romeo

St. Romanus was born in what is now France. He was 35 when he entered a monastery in Lyons. Not finding the life severe enough, he left to become a hermit in a remote area. Later he was joined by his brother and then a sister, and three monasteries were founded by them. He is said to have worked many miracles. One day he met two lepers on the road and embraced them. After he had gone on, the lepers were surprised to see that they had been healed and were no longer disfigured. He died about 463. He is prayed to for people with mental illness.

# Ronald (Scottish form of Reginald,  Aug. 20
*Teutonic:* Strong Judgment)

## Other Forms: Ronaldo, Aldo

St. Ronald was a British chieftain of Orkney. He built the Cathedral of St. Magnus in Kirkwall. He was killed by rebels in 1158. Because of the holiness of his life, many miracles are said to have taken place in his name following his death.

# Rudolph (*Teutonic:* Famous Wolf)

## Other Forms: Rolfe, Rodolfo, Rodolphus, Rudolf

Blessed Rudolf was the son of the Duke of Atri, Spain, who joined the Jesuit Society at the age of 18. After his ordination, he was sent to preach the Gospel in the region of Agra, India. Later he was transferred to an area north of Bombay. Here the Hindus gave great opposition. Blessed Rudolf decided to build a church in the village of Cuncolim, where the opposition was the strongest. Together with some other Jesuits and Indian laymen, he went there on July 15, 1583. Hindus ambushed them, killing the members of the party with arrows.

# Rupert *(Teutonic:* Bright Flame) Mar. 27

### Other Forms: Robert (see), Ruprecht

St. Rupert was a French priest who was appointed Bishop of Worms, Germany. Some people in power resented him and drove him from his see. He then preached Christianity in Bavaria and Upper Germany, making many converts. With this success he established his see at what is now Salzburg. Here he died on Easter Sunday, 718.

# Salvatore *(Latin:* Savior)

### Other Forms: Salvador, Salvator

This name is from the title given to Our Lord Jesus Christ, Savior, and most people who receive this name have been given it in honor of Jesus. It can be celebrated on any feast of Our Lord but is most appropriate at Easter.

SALVATOR OF HORTA (Mar. 18)

St. Salvator of Horta is one of the great wonder workers of the Church. He began life as a shepherd, then became a shoemaker, and finally a Franciscan Brother. As a Brother he served as a cook and porter. He is reputed to have had great healing powers, working many miracles. People came from all over Spain to seek his aid. He died in 1567. He is a patron of shoemakers.

# Samuel *(Hebrew:* Asked of the Lord) Aug. 20

### Another Form: Samuele

Samuel was one of the great prophets of the Old Testament, and you can read about him in the First Book of Kings. His mother, Anna, had long been childless, and she promised God that if He gave her a son she would dedicate him to His work. God heard her prayer, and Samuel was born. Anna took Samuel, while still a boy, to the high priest, Eli, to serve him and be educated. It was while serving Eli that Samuel was called by God to be His prophet. Samuel became a Judge of Israel, selected Saul to be King, and when he failed, replaced him with the great King David.

ST. THOMAS

# Sebastian (*Greek:* Venerable)          Jan. 20

Sebastian was born in Milan and went to Rome to enlist in the army, where he hoped he could help fellow Christians who were being persecuted. He first saved the brothers Marcus and Marcellinus, who had been condemned to death, by speaking so fervently of Christ that he converted the jailer, the clerk of the prefecture, the parents of the condemned men and sixteen prisoners. These conversions led to the conversion of the governor of Rome, who released the prisoners. During this time Sebastian was such a good soldier that Emperor Diocletian made him a captain of the Praetorian Guard. He was finally discovered and delivered up to the archers. When arrows failed to kill him, he was beaten to death and his body thrown into a sewer. He died about 288 A.D.

# Sigmund (*Teutonic:* Victorious Protector)          May 1

### Other Forms: Siegmund, Sigismondo, Sigismund

Sigmund is a diminutive form of Sigismund, a king of Burgundy (France). He ruled for but one year, during which time he allowed his son to be put to death. Filled with remorse, he resigned as king and founded a monastery, to which he retired to live a life of penance. He was seized by an enemy chieftain and put to death in 524. He is honored as a martyr, and a shrine was built to his memory in Bohemia (Prague).

# Simon (*Hebrew:* Obedient)          Oct. 28

### Other Forms: Simeon, Simone

St. Simon was an Apostle who was also known as The Zealot to differ him from St. Simon Peter, who had the same first name until Jesus changed it. He was a native of Cana and may have been a member of the political-religious group called Zealots, or perhaps he got the name from his personal zeal. Some years ago there was a story speculating that St. Simon was the bridegroom for whom Jesus turned water into wine, but there is no indication of such a connection in the Gospels. Tradition says he preached the Gospel in Persia and was martyred there.

Other saints with this name:

St. Simon of Cyrene (Palestine) *Dec. 1*
St. Simeon of Jerusalem (*Feb. 18*)
St. Simon Stock (England) *May 16*
St. Simeon Stylites (Syria) *Jan. 5*

# Stanislaus (Slavic: Military Glory)　　　　Apr. 11

## Other Forms: Stanislao, Stanislas, Stanley

St. Stanislaus is honored as a bishop and martyr. He was born in Poland and educated at the University of Paris. He became bishop at a time Poland was ruled by King Boleslaus, a mighty warrior whose personal life was very sinful. Stanislaus threatened to excommunicate the king unless he remedied his evil ways. For a time the king seemed to reform, but after defeating the Russians at Kiev, Boleslaus returned home victorious and popular, thinking he was bigger than the Church. Once again he returned to his evil life. Stanislaus gave him several warnings and then for the good of souls excommunicated him. The king refused to accept the excommunication and turned up for Mass. St. Stanislaus refused to celebrate Mass in the cathedral but went to a small church outside the city. Boleslaus followed him there and ordered his soldiers to arrest the bishop. When they held back because of respect, Boleslaus took his sword and split the saint's head open. The year was 1079.

Another saint with this name:

St. Stanislaus Kostka (Poland) *Aug. 15*

# Stephen (Greek: Crowned)

## Other Forms: Esteban, Stefan, Stefano, Stefen, Stephan, Steven, Sven

ST. STEPHEN MARTYR　　　　　　　　　　　　　　　(Dec. 26)

St. Stephen is the first martyr of the Church, patron of smelters and stonecutters. He was a disciple in the early Church who was selected to become a deacon. The Acts of the Apostles describes him as a man "full of grace and power, who did great wonders and signs among the people." He debated with the Jews in their synagogues, and when they could not stand up against his wisdom, they accused him falsely to the chief priests. He was arrested and taken before the Jewish council. The Book of Acts records his sermon before the council. The Jews, however, stopped up their ears, dragged him outside the walls, and stoned him. As they were stoning him, Stephen prayed: "Lord Jesus, receive my spirit" and "Lord, do not hold this sin against them." So praying, he died. Among those at the stoning was a man named Saul, who later was to be converted and become St. Paul.

When St. Stephen became a Christian, he took for his baptismal name that of the first martyr. He was crowned King of Hungary in the year 1000 when he was twenty years old. He was a just king who strove to convert his subjects to the Church, earning from the pope the title of Apostolic King. He dedicated his country to the Blessed Virgin. St. Stephen died in 1038, and his crown is the most precious relic in Hungary today.


# Terence (*Latin:* Smooth)                              Apr. 10

### Other Forms: Terrence, Terry


St. Terence was a martyr who died in Carthage during the persecution of Decius, about 250. Nothing else is known of him.


# Thaddeus (*Aramaic:* Wise)                             Oct. 28


Thaddeus is another name for St. Jude the Apostle (*see*), who is known as Jude Thaddeus.


# Theodore (*Greek:* God's Gift)                         Feb. 7

### Other Forms: Feodor, Tad, Teodoro, Theo, Theodotius


Theodore was a member of a Roman legion stationed in the East. He was denounced as a Christian. Theodore was given his release with a warning. Despite this, he set fire to a pagan temple and was again arrested. This time Theodore was ordered to deny his Christian faith. When he refused, he was tortured by having his flesh torn. Still refusing to recant, he was put to death by being burned about the year 319.

*ST. VINCENT DE PAUL*

# Thomas *Aramaic:* Twin)

## Other Forms: Tomas, Tommaso

### THOMAS THE APOSTLE (July 3)

When Jesus was preparing to return to the vicinity of Jerusalem the last time before His death, it was Thomas who exclaimed to the other Apostles, "Let us also go and die with Him." Thomas, also called Didymus, The Twin, was not with the other Apostles when Jesus appeared to them after the Resurrection. When they told him about their experience, Thomas refused to believe, saying, "Unless I place my finger in the mark of the nails, and my hand in His side, I will not believe." Eight days later Jesus appeared again and called Thomas to put his finger in the nail holes and his hand in His side, adding: "Do not be faithless but believing." Thomas answered: "My Lord and my God." According to tradition Thomas preached the Gospel as far away as India where he was martyred. He is the patron of architects and masons.

### ST. THOMAS AQUINAS (Jan. 28)

St. Thomas Aquinas is a Doctor (Teacher) of the Church and patron of Catholic schools. He became a Dominican friar, studied under St. Albert the Great, and taught in universities in Cologne, Bologna, and Paris. He has been called the Church's most outstanding writer and teacher of philosophy and theology, leaving behind a large library of writings. He died on the way to the Council of Lyons in 1369.

### ST. THOMAS BECKET (Dec. 29)

Born in London, Thomas, was selected by Henry II to be his chancellor of England. He lived in luxury and power, a close friend and confidant of the king. When the episcopal see of Canterbury became vacant, Henry named his friend to be the archbishop. Thomas was ordained a priest and consecrated a bishop. He immediately changed his life from luxury to austerity. He felt that there was a conflict of interest between his roles as leading churchman and chancellor, so he resigned the latter post, to the anger of Henry. He further angered Henry by siding with the pope in a dispute with the king. Henry sent him into exile. When he was permitted to return, Henry counted on his friendship and obedience. But again Thomas protected the interests of the Church and the pope. "Won't someone rid me of this insolent priest?" Henry exclaimed in anger. Some henchmen heard him and went to the cathedral, where they found Thomas at prayer and there in 1170 murdered him.

### ST. THOMAS MORE (June 22)

St. Thomas More was the chancellor of England under King Henry VIII. When the king broke with the pope because he would not be granted a divorce, Thomas refused to join the new Church of England. He was tried for treason and found guilty. Condemned with beheading, Thomas joked with his executioners, even removing his beard from the execution block, saying that it had done nothing wrong and didn't deserve to be cut. St. Thomas was an educated and humorous man who had a deep spirituality and loyalty to the papacy. He died in 1535.

# Timothy (*Greek:* God Fearing) Jan. 26

### Other Forms: Timoteo, Timotheus

Timothy was a convert of St. Paul who later became his close friend and companion. Two letters that St. Paul wrote to his beloved Timothy can be found in the New Testament. Timothy traveled with Paul through the Near East, to Greece and Rome. He also took missionary journeys alone. St. Paul charged him: "Preach the word, be urgent in season and out of season, convince, rebuke, and exhort." In his last letter to Timothy, Paul writes that he is at the point of being sacrificed, saying, "I have fought the good fight, I have finished the race, I have kept the faith." He urges Timothy to hurry to him before winter comes. Later Timothy became a bishop of the Church at Ephesus, and tradition says that he was stoned to death during a pagan feast.

# Titus (*Latin:* Safe) Jan. 4

### Another Form: Tito

St. Titus was a gentile convert of St. Paul the Apostle. He assisted Paul in his work of conversion. St. Paul sent him to both Corinth and Crete to settle problems in the churches there. St. Paul wrote a letter to him which is contained in the New Testament (Epistle to Titus). He is honored as the first bishop of the Island of Crete. He died there about the end of the first century.

# Tobias (*Hebrew:* Goodness of God) Nov. 2

### Other Forms: Tobia, Tobiah, Tobit

St. Tobias was a Christian soldier in the army of the Emperor Licinius who was stationed in Armenia. When the soldiers were ordered to take part in a sacrifice to pagan gods, Tobias and some other Christians refused. They were burned at the stake for their refusal about the year 315. (There is also a Biblical figure named Tobias, and his story can be read in the Book of Tobit.)

*ST. WENCESLAUS*

# Urban *(Latin:* Man of the City)      May 25

### Other Forms: Urbano, Urbanus

Urban is the name for a number of popes, bishops and martyrs. The first pope who is a saint with this name is Pope St. Urban I, who is honored as a martyr. He succeeded St. Callistus as pope in 223 and ruled the Church during a period of persecution, working to help those who were arrested. Among the martyrs he helped was St. Cecilia. He died in 230.

# Valerius *(Latin:* Valiant)      Feb. 14

### Other Forms: Balentin, Valens, Valentine, Valentino, Valentinus, Valerian, Valeriano, Valerio

Valerius, or Valentine, was a priest in Rome. He was arrested and taken before the Emperor Claudius the Goth, to whom he confessed his faith and denounced the pagan gods Jupiter and Mercury. He was turned over to a magistrate named Asterius, who had a blind daughter. Valentine converted Asterius and his family when he restored sight to the blind girl. He was reported again to the emperor for these conversions, and Claudius ordered him decapitated on the Flaminian Way about 270. Pope Nicholas I built a church in his honor, and it became a place of pilgrimage. He is the patron of engaged couples.

# Victor *(Latin:* Winner)      July 21

### Other Forms: Victorio, Vittorio

Victor was an officer in the army stationed in Marseilles. When Maximianus Herculius arrived in the city, the Christians were very worried because that general had just massacred the Thebian Legion for being Christian. Victor was exhorting his Christian soldiers to be firm when he was caught in the act. He was taken before the prefects of the legion, who told him to be faithful to the gods and not to a dead man named Jesus. The prefects sent him to Maximianus, who ordered him to be dragged through the streets of the city, tortured on the rack, and finally crushed to death under a millstone. He died about 287. He is the patron of cabinetmakers and is invoked against lightning.

# Vincent (*Latin:* Conquering)

## Other Forms: Vincente, Vincentius, Vincenzo

### ST. VINCENT THE DEACON (Jan. 22)

St. Vincent is a martyr who has had great popularity throughout Europe. He was a deacon who was assistant to the Bishop Valerius in what is now Spain. When the persecutions of Diocletian began, the Roman governor of the province had Valerius and Vincent arrested. Because the bishop was old, Vincent asked to speak for him. This made the governor angry. He ordered that Vincent's flesh be cut with iron hooks and then that the deacon be roasted over a slow fire. Vincent prayed and sang psalms until he died. He is the patron of winegrowers. He died about 305.

### ST. VINCENT FERRER (Apr. 5)

St. Vincent Ferrer was born in Valencia, Spain, and took his name from the deacon-martyr St. Vincent, who had been put to death there by the Romans. He entered the Dominican order and soon became noted for his preaching and faith healing, working many miracles. His preaching took him throughout Spain, France, Switzerland, and Italy. He is reputed to have converted many lukewarm Catholics. He died in 1419. He is the patron of construction workers.

### ST. VINCENT DE PAUL (Sept. 27)

One of the great figures of the French Church, St. Vincent was born into a laboring class family in the south of France about 1580. As a boy he tended sheep and did farm chores. Because he was intelligent and wished to become a priest, his father resolved to help him and sold two oxen to pay for his education. He became a priest and strove for worldly honors. On a journey along the coast of France, he was captured by Barbary (Moslem) pirates and taken as prisoner to Tunis. He escaped for a return to France and honors, becoming almoner of the queen and holder of many benefices. Then in 1617 he renounced all his honors and became a great saint and apostle. To the rich and poor, he was simply known as Monsieur Vincent. He labored for the galley slaves and the poor. He founded the Vincentian Order and the Sisters of Charity. His charities became a model for the whole Church. He died in Paris, Sept. 27, 1737.

# Vladimir (*Slovak:* World Ruler) July 15

St. Vladimir was baptized in 987 when he was king of an area that is now part of Russia. He enlarged his kingdom by recovering territory from the Poles, defeating the Bulgars along the Volga River, and capturing territories in the north as far as Finland. At the same time he brought Christian missioners from Byzantium (Constantinople) and Germany. He destroyed paganism in the area and brought whole populations into the Church.

# Walter *(Teutonic:* Strong Warrior) Apr. 8

## Other Forms: Gualthieri, Walther

St. Walter was born in Picardy, France. He is the patron saint of prisoners, because when he was a novice studying to be a monk, he smuggled bread in to a peasant who was being held a prisoner and at night entered the man's cell to free him from his chains. He was later elected abbot of his monastery, much against his will. Several times he tried to escape his role of abbot, once retiring to the Abbey of Cluny and again making a retreat into the forests. Each time his holiness attracted crowds and he was discovered. Finally, Pope Gregory VII ordered him to fulfill his duties as abbot, which he did for the remainder of his life. He died about 1095.

# Wenceslaus *(Slavic:* Great Glory) Sept. 28

## Other Forms: Vinceslao, Wenceslas

Wenceslaus was thirteen when his father, the King of Bohemia, died. His mother, a pagan, ruled until he became eighteen. Wenceslaus was trained in Christianity by his grandmother. When he became king, he ended the persecution of the Christians, recalled exiled priests, built churches, and is said to have ground the wheat and made the wine to be used at the Eucharist. Wenceslaus invited his pagan brother, Boleslaus, to join him in celebrating the feast of Sts. Cosmas and Damian. On the way to Mass, Boleslaus had his brother murdered. The people proclaimed Wenceslaus a martyr and he is honored as the patron of Bohemia. He died in 935.

# Wilfrid *(Old English:* Firm Peace) Oct. 12

St. Wilfrid was a famous bishop of the Anglo-Saxon Church. He became the Archbishop of York and was several times exiled from England because he defended the Church against the king. During his banishments he went to Rome and preached the faith in Europe. He is one of the apostles of Holland and is honored on the Isle of Wight. He died in 709.

# William (*Teutonic:* Strong Helmet) June 25

**Other Forms: Guglielmo, Guiliermo, Guillaume, Wilhelm, Willis**

St. William was born in the Piedmont area of Italy. From the time he was a boy he lived a life of penance. He made the famous pilgrimage to the shrine of St. James in Spain on his bare feet. He founded a number of monasteries for men and women. He died in 1142.


# Xavier (*Arabic:* Bright) Dec. 3

A name given in honor of St. Francis Xavier (see), patron of the missions.


# Zachary (*Hebrew:* Remembered by God) Nov. 5

**Other Forms: Zaccaria, Zacharias, Zechariah**

St. Zachary was the father of St. John the Baptist and the husband of St. Elizabeth. He and his wife lived near Jerusalem. He was a priest who took his turn serving in the Temple. One day while on duty, he had a vision of an angel who told him that he was to have a son whom he should name John. After the vision, he was struck dumb, and he did not regain his speech until after John was born and it came time to name the child. When he was able to speak again, he uttered the beautiful Benedictus prayer which is still part of our liturgy. Zachary's story can be read in the first chapter of St. Luke's Gospel.

# Part Two:

# Names in This Book

There are thousands of saints who are not in this book. However, if your name is not listed below, there is a good chance your name is not a saint's name. It may be a partial name or nickname; very few such names are listed here. If your given name is Thom or Tom, Dick or Rick, Hal or Harry, you should look under Thomas, Richard, Harold or Henry. Your first name may be a family name, a made-up name, or a name from popular, non-Christian mythology. In this case you could "adopt" a patron saint whose name sounds like yours.

112

114

115

117